The Harlem Renaissance

The Harlem Renaissance

An Annotated Reference Guide
for
Student Research

Marie E. Rodgers

1998
Libraries Unlimited, Inc.
Englewood, Colorado

Libraries Unlimited, Inc.
P.O. Box 6633
Englewood, CO 80155-6633
1-800-237-6124
www.lu.com

Production Editor: Kay Mariea
Copy Editor: Jan Krygier
Proofreader: Louise Tonneson
Indexer: Linda Bentley
Interior Design and Typesetting: Judy Gay Matthews

Library of Congress Cataloging-in-Publication Data

Rodgers, Marie E.
    The Harlem Renaissance : an annotated reference guide
for student research / Marie E. Rodgers.
    xvii, 139 p.   17x25 cm.
    Includes bibliographical references and index.
    ISBN 1-56308-580-1
    1. Harlem Renaissance--Bibliography.   2. Afro-American
arts--New York (State)--New York--Bibliography.   I. Title.
Z5956.A47R64   1998
[NX512.3.A35]
016.700'89'96073007471--dc21   97-46660
                                                      CIP

Dedication

Chapter 1 is dedicated to Elana Elster
Chapter 6 is dedicated to Cherie Lazear
Chapter 8 is dedicated to Shannon Rodgers
Chapter 12 is dedicated to Mary Andrews
Chapter 13 is dedicated to Brian Rodgers
Chapter 15 is dedicated to Sam
Chapter 17 is dedicated to Bernard Moody and Timothy Heyward
Chapter 19 is dedicated to Zoraida Diaz
Chapter 20 is dedicated to Michelle L. Cushner
The index is dedicated to Donald E. Westlake

Contents

Part I

Historical and Biographical References

Part II

Notable Contributors

Part III

Literature and Writing

Part IV

Visual Arts

PART V

THE PERFORMING ARTS

PART VI

SPORTS AND ENTERTAINMENT

Figures

PREFACE

My interest in jazz led to my interest in this topic. I became a jazz fan at the age of 14 when I heard Thelonius Monk on the radio. As an avid reader and listener, I wanted to find everything I could that had been written about jazz. That led to my discovery of Langston Hughes. I first read his poetry, and then I discovered his autobiography at the public library. It was the first thick book I read as a teenager. It was also my introduction to the Harlem Renaissance. Then, about five years ago, I went to work as a librarian in a public school in Harlem. My colleagues and I visited a neighborhood restaurant and learned that an employee there had been a dancer at the Cotton Club. She told us about the people she had met and what the nightlife was like in Harlem during its heyday. My interest increased even more.

At the same time, I was completing an M.L.S. degree; a thesis loomed in the near future. I knew that I wanted to research the Harlem Renaissance. As I began to gather material, it became clear that the students I worked with had little or no knowledge of that period; at best, a few knew that it had something to do with Black writers. I began to look at social studies textbooks and search for materials for students. Not much could be found. Fortunately, in the past five years, this has changed somewhat.

I hope this guide will provide students with a background concerning the era and lead them to explore it further. Most of all, I hope that all students gain an awareness and understanding of all the elements that contributed to the Harlem Renaissance.

Acknowledgments

The bulk of the research for this work was completed at the Schomburg Center for Research in Black Culture of the New York Public Library. All photographs for this work were obtained from the library's Photographs and Prints Division. The Schomburg Center is truly a wonderful place. I would like to thank the staff, in particular Ennis Winston Jr., Anthony Toussaint, Melvin Voyd, and Oneida Mitchell, for their kind assistance.

I am also grateful to John C. Revi, who supplied me with information which greatly increased my computer literacy.

Thanks also to the staff of Libraries Unlimited, including Ron Maas, General Manager; Kay Mariea, Production Editor; Stacy Ennis Chisholm, Author Relations Coordinator; and Jan Krygier, Copy Editor.

INTRODUCTION

Harlem Renaissance is a term that has been used to define a period of flowering, exploration, and flourishing of the arts among African American writers and artists from roughly 1920 to 1933. It is often seen as a collaboration by a select few. This interpretation is especially evident in social studies textbooks, which often devote as little as a paragraph to the entire era. Researchers and scholars may have a broader base of knowledge, but the average reader or student has limited knowledge of the sum or of the parts that created the Harlem Renaissance.

As a result, a study of the Harlem Renaissance often focuses only on one aspect of it: artistic expression. Studying the social history of the time period, however, is important for several reasons. Doing so will provide a more solid base of understanding for the reader. It will also provide a point of view other than that of the purely artistic or the purely critical. A more enlightened understanding of the social history of the time period also provides new insight into the artist's or writer's work. The climate of life in Harlem at the time contributed greatly to the Harlem Renaissance, which was based on equality, pride within a race, and recognition for Blacks in the United States. Because Langston Hughes is widely known, many readers may be aware that his work especially reflects the context of the Harlem community at that time. However, this is true of most other writers and artists as well. When all factors contributing to the Renaissance are recognized, the period emerges as more than a simple literary or artistic movement. It is a historic period of the community of Harlem, a time of many significant social, political, and cultural accomplishments. Not only did these accomplishments affect Harlem and African Americans, they also affected culture and race in America. For that reason alone, the period deserves to be studied in greater depth at the high school level. This book can assist in such a study.

Selection Criteria

Many of the titles in this book are primary works about the Harlem Renaissance. Others center on particular individuals who were a part of the era. Most works cited in this book have been published within the last 15 years. However, there are exceptions. Older books still in print that offer relevant information are included, as well as books out of print (provided that they offer valuable information not found elsewhere). Note that not all works out of print will include prices.

All titles chosen for inclusion in this book deal specifically with some aspect of the Harlem Renaissance, even if it is only within a section or chapter; such works are included because the information they provide is valuable and relevant.

Although several sources may appear within some topics or subjects, such lists are not comprehensive. Several biographies on one subject may be included for a number of reasons—the age of the intended audience may vary; autobiographies and biographies are likely to have different perspectives; and later works often contain new material not found in earlier works.

This book does not include works of fiction. Many book lists, however, contain bibliographies that do list fiction titles. Nor does it include works written in a language other than English. Rare books, pamphlets, and periodicals are omitted, with one exception. Because this book is designed for young adult students, it does not contain esoteric works. Some scholarly works have been included when they are written at a level appropriate for high school students.

Audience

This book has been written for students in grades 7 through 12. Obviously, not all works will be appropriate for use by all students. Thus, a recommended audience is noted in each annotation. Recommendations indicate that the work is appropriate for specific grade levels. Whenever possible, grade levels determined by publishers were used. Otherwise, grade levels were determined by the author based on subject matter, length of the work, and accessibility of the source.

Annotations

Annotations are descriptive of the organization and content of the work. Each annotation also provides information on how the work is relevant to the Harlem Renaissance. Finally, recommendations as to the intended or appropriate audience are made.

For a variety of reasons, some sources appear in more than one chapter of this book. Walter White and Paul Robeson, for example, were both political activists, but they also contributed to the Harlem Renaissance in other ways. Works related to them are listed in each relevant section. Thus, people interested in Walter White as a novelist will want to refer to chapter 6,

"Literature," for works related to that aspect of his career. Works related to Paul Robeson can be found in both chapter 14, "Classical and Concert Music," and in chapter 10, "Film," because he was active in both areas. Finally, some sources, such as Bruce Kellner's *The Harlem Renaissance: A Historical Dictionary of the Era*, contain a wealth of information not often found in other sources. Consequently, these works are cited in several sections.

Nonprint Materials

The audiocassette and videocassette tapes included here are merely a sampling of what is available. All of the audiocassettes listed were recorded during the Harlem Renaissance. They are included here to provide students with authentic sounds of the 1920s and 1930s. They are not necessarily definitive samples of music of the era.

The videocassettes were chosen for their historical significance and their relevance for classroom use. As with the audiocassette tapes, the videotapes are meant to supplement classroom instruction, not replace it.

There is a definite need for young adult material that presents social, historical, and political aspects of life in Harlem during its Renaissance. This guide addresses that need. Teachers who wish to supplement their texts will find this guide useful in locating information. Librarians can use this book to help locate and compile materials on the Harlem Renaissance. The lists in this book will assist anyone who wishes to locate more about specific topics related to the Harlem Renaissance.

Part I

Historical and Biographical References

Fig. 1.1.
135th St. and Lenox Avenue, 1919 (Schomburg Center, NYPL).

Historical Overview

The Harlem Renaissance did not just happen. Many factors contributed to it. It is important to identify these factors so that the reader understands the real essence of the movement. It was more than an artistic or literary movement; it was a cultural movement, a call for equality and recognition for African Americans. It is difficult to pinpoint the exact beginning of the Harlem Renaissance. Depending on which reference one is reading, several "beginnings" can be identified. Among them are the 1921 opening of *Shuffle Along*, the first Broadway musical written, produced, directed, choreographed, and cast entirely by African Americans; the 1924 Civic Club dinner, which was organized by Charles S. Johnson and attended by several young African American authors; and the 1925 publication of Alain Locke's book *The New Negro*, an anthology of works by African American authors. Although these events are all significant, there were many more contributing factors to the Harlem Renaissance.

Disillusionment

In 1919, soldiers returned home from the Great War, World War I. Many Black and White veterans became disillusioned by the lack of economic opportunity. However, unrest had been brewing among African American soldiers even before then. Although they were needed to fight the war and were expected to do their duty, African American soldiers were mistreated, did not receive the training that Whites had received, and were segregated. To make matters worse, they were not given the hero status they deserved. Other factors, such as an increase in lynchings and agricultural failure in the South, added to the racial unrest. Finally, in the summer of 1919, race riots broke out in 25 cities in the United States. The time was right for a new movement. For some, that movement was Marcus Garvey's "Back to Africa" philosophy. For others, it was the philosophy of W. E. B. Du Bois, who sought social justice and advocated higher education as a means to equality.

THE GREAT MIGRATION

Most of those who helped shape the Harlem Renaissance were not native Harlemites; nor was Harlem originally an African American community. Many African Americans arrived in New York City as part of the Great Migration, which began around 1916 and continued through the era of the Harlem Renaissance. They often settled in Harlem, where Whites were still living.

Before the Great Migration, the majority of African Americans resided in the South. Many factors led to the movement North in the years just prior to the Harlem Renaissance. Racism and little or no economic opportunity made life difficult and intolerable for many rural Southern Blacks. U.S. involvement in World War I affected the Northern economy in ways that were beneficial to African Americans. Because of the war, immigration declined sharply, and the war itself created an economic boom for workers. These two factors presented job opportunities in northern cities for everyone, including African Americans. They left the South by the hundreds of thousands to take advantage of these opportunities and to escape racism and poverty. Those from Southern states along the eastern seaboard settled in Philadelphia, Baltimore, and Washington, D.C., as well as in New York. By the time of the Harlem Renaissance, more African Americans living in New York resided in Harlem than in any other section of the city.

MECCA FOR THE ARTS

It is true that the publication of Alain Locke's book *The New Negro* contributed greatly to the Harlem Renaissance. In fact, the term "New Negro" became the label used to identify urban, educated African Americans of the 1920s. However, the fact that most publishing companies were located in Manhattan also played a part in the influx of African American writers to New York, which was and is also a major center for those involved in theater, art, and music.

The literary world opened its arms to African American writers because of Carl Van Vechten's efforts and connections to the publishing world. Van Vechten, a wealthy dilettante, had at one time been a music critic for *The New York Times*. In addition to Van Vechten's efforts, on March 21, 1924, the Civic Club, one of the few clubs open to African Americans at the time, held a dinner that brought many African American writers to the attention of White publishers. Never before had so many Black writers had the opportunity to be published and read by the mainstream of American society.

Everything seemed to be happening at once. The musical show *Shuffle Along* was a huge success on Broadway. It was soon followed by shows such as *Runnin' Wild* and musical revues performed at Harlem nightclubs like the Cotton Club and Connie's Inn. African themes in sculpture and art were popular with

Blacks and Whites alike. Dances like the Charleston, originated by African Americans, also became the rage among Whites, who flocked uptown to see and learn the latest dances at the Savoy Ballroom. Jazz gained wide recognition and was more popular than ever among both Blacks and Whites. Blues, originally African American regional music of the South brought North with the Great Migration, also enjoyed a wide audience of Black and White fans. Harlem nightclubs, such as the Cotton Club, Tillie's Chicken Shack, and Pod's and Jerry's, were the places to go for jazz, blues, and fabulous floor shows. Harlem was "in."

Not only were the artistic expressions of Black Americans recognized, political leaders such as Marcus Garvey, A. Philip Randolph, and W. E. B. Du Bois also found recognition. Garvey, a Jamaican immigrant, rose from street corner politician to leader of the Universal Negro Improvement Association, one of the most powerful African American groups of the era. At the same time, A. Philip Randolph championed the rights of Black workers in labor unions.

W. E. B. Du Bois, a true intellectual, identified what he called "The Talented Tenth," the educated upper class of African Americans, who were, in a sense, cultural leaders of the race. It would be the Talented Tenth, he said, who would enable the race to rise above the vulgar and mundane and put an end to negative stereotypes of Blacks as uneducated and lacking in culture. Many African Americans felt that Du Bois's concept of identifying the top 10 percent of his race as cultured and educated was elitist. However, during the 1920s, more African Americans achieved professional status than ever before.

It seemed that, for the first time, the mainstream was open to African Americans. Literature, music, and art of Black Americans received deserved recognition and respectability. African American political leaders had a voice, and mainstream Americans listened to them.

Day-to-day life in Harlem was, however, a far cry from that of the "New Negro" or of the wealthy White Manhattanites who traveled uptown nightly for an exotic evening of fun. Few businesses were owned by Blacks. Harlem rents were far above what the average person could afford. Several people often shared a flat, making for cramped quarters. Sharing a flat, however, worked well for those who worked different hours, since sleeping shifts could be alternated. "Rent parties" were fun and an inexpensive night out, but in reality, the admission charged to guests was a means of raising money to pay the exorbitant rent. Many average, working-class African Americans could not have afforded an evening at the Cotton Club even if their admittance had been permitted. The money that flowed into Harlem did not benefit the community; it went into the pockets of absentee landlords and business owners, most of whom were White. For the average working man, life in Harlem was a far cry from that of the Talented Tenth. Under the glittering surface, Harlem was suffering.

Decline

The Harlem Renaissance ended as it began. Just as a combination of factors heralded its beginning, several events contributed to its decline. The stock market crash of 1929 greatly affected the movement. Patrons no longer had the means or the desire to extend their wealth to unknown artists and writers. As the Great Depression spread across the country, frivolity and lavish spending were replaced by unemployment and poverty. Harlem, itself, had fallen into a decline. Many working-class families paid higher rents than their counterparts in other areas of Manhattan. By the early 1930s, Harlem was viewed as a slum. The Cotton Club had moved to midtown Manhattan. Economic decay set in everywhere.

Many of the influential participants of the movement left Harlem to pursue other endeavors. Charles S. Johnson and James Weldon Johnson both left Harlem for faculty positions at Fisk University in Nashville, Tennessee. Alain Locke, who was already on the faculty of Howard University in Washington, D.C., found less and less opportunity to travel to Harlem. Jessie Fauset traded her position at *The Crisis* for marriage. By 1934, the Harlem Renaissance had ended forever in spirit; only the achievements of those associated with it would remain. Fortunately, many artifacts of the era had already been collected.

Arthur Schomburg and the 135th Street Library

Arthur Schomburg was born in Puerto Rico in 1874. He studied Black literature in college and devoted his professional life to promoting Black culture. He lived and worked in Harlem during the Renaissance, where he published many articles and contributed to an anthology of works by Black writers called *The New Negro*, Alain Locke's defining work on the era. By 1926, Schomburg had collected thousands of books, manuscripts, and other materials related to Black culture, which he donated to the 135th Street branch of the New York Public Library, already a center for cultural activities. The collection has expanded and is housed next door to the library. It is the largest collection on Black culture in America and bears his name: The Schomburg Center for Research in Black Culture.

Each of the following references offers a significant historical perspective on the Harlem Renaissance. Several sources were written specifically about the Harlem Renaissance; others of a more general nature have a worthwhile section that provides an in-depth discussion of the historical perspective of the era. Bruce Kellner's and David Levering Lewis's works focus entirely on the Harlem Renaissance. Steven Watson's newer work, part of the Circles of the 20th Century series, is also an excellent resource.

BiblioqRaphy

Cowan, Tom, and Jack Maguire. **Timelines of African American History: 500 Years of Black Achievement**. New York: Roundtable Press/Perigee Books, 1994. 368p. $15.00. ISBN 0-399-52127-5.

This chronological arrangement of significant events in African American history divides each year into categories, such as "Politics," "Civil Rights," "Literature," "Performing Arts," and "Sports," depending on which significant events occurred within that year. Sidebar sections on several pages include pertinent information for each year; topics related to the Harlem Renaissance include "The National Urban League" and "A. Philip Randolph." Along the bottom of each page is a section, "Contemporary Events," which provides information on national events for the year. This is a good source for historical information on African Americans; it is both informative and fun to browse. A bibliography and index are also included. Recommended for grades 7 through 12 and above.

Douglas, Ann. **Terrible Honesty: Mongrel Manhattan in the 1920s**. New York: Farrar, Straus & Giroux, 1995. 610p. $25.00. ISBN 0-374-11620-2.

Douglas's introduction traces the history of New York City and provides details on all of the elements that contributed to its rise during the Harlem Renaissance. Douglas provides a psychological perspective to her work by explaining the role of William James and Sigmund Freud in the newfound modernism of the 1920s. The book is based on the lives and work of 120 New Yorkers. Douglas devotes chapters to the arts in New York City and the system of patronage. She also devotes an entire section to Harlem. Written in narrative, the book is rich in detail, which makes it a fascinating study of the era and an excellent source of information. Included are a selective bibliography and discography. Recommended for grades 10 through 12 and above.

Douglas, Melvin L. **Black Winners: History of Springarn Medalists 1915–1983**. Atlanta, GA: DARE Books, 1984. 160p. $7.95. ISBN 0-912444-31-2.

Many of those active in the Harlem Renaissance won the Springarn Medal. The medal was instituted by Joel Elias Springarn to honor African American achievements. Springarn made financial arrangements that would ensure continuation of awards through perpetuity.

Douglas has compiled winners from 1915 through 1983, arranging the information by decade. The book begins with a brief background of the medal. Douglas then provides biographical sketches of each medalist. Information on each recipient includes dates of birth and death, field of endeavor, contribution, and education. Medalists related to the Harlem Renaissance include W. E. B. Du Bois, Roland Hayes, James Weldon Johnson, Walter White, Marian Anderson, Paul Robeson, A. Philip Randolph, Duke Ellington, and Langston Hughes. The medal is awarded for lifetime achievement; therefore, many of them were honored decades after their initial achievements. Douglas also includes black-and-white illustrations; a bibliography; a list of winners, which includes year, field, and presenter; and tables listing distribution of winners by birthplace and field of endeavor. Those interested in obtaining more specific information about each winner will need to consult other sources because this source focuses specifically on Springarn Medal winners and is written especially for grades 7 through 10. Bibliographical sketches are brief.

Estell, Kenneth, ed. **Reference Library of Black America**. Vol. 1 of Chronology Series. Detroit, MI: Gale Research, 1993. 1600p. $179.00. ISBN 0-685-49222-2.

An essay focusing on historical perspectives of African American history opens this volume. There is also an extensive bibliography at the end of the volume. It includes sections, such as "African American Firsts" and "African American Landmarks." Many entries in these sections are linked to the Harlem Renaissance. It is interesting to see that many African American "firsts" occurred during the Harlem Renaissance. There are also several maps and illustrations. Formerly *The Negro Almanac*, this is a highly regarded reference tool for students in grades 7 through 12.

Gardiner, Harry. "A Visit with Margaret Perry." **Cobblestone** 12, no. 2 (February 1991): 14–17.

Perry is highly respected for her work as an author of several books about the Harlem Renaissance. Here, Perry is interviewed by Harry Gardiner. The interview, presented in a question-and-answer format, covers such topics as why the Renaissance happened, lesser-known personalities, and what Perry sees as the legacy of the Renaissance. This article is brief, but it contains much information as seen through the eyes of a historian. Although appearing in a publication for younger students, the article is also appropriate for grades 7 through 10.

Grant, Joanne. "The 20th Century." In **Black Protest: History, Documents and Analyses, 1619 to the Present**. 2d ed. Black History Titles Series. New York: Fawcett Premier, 1991. 507p. $4.95. ISBN 0-449-30044-7.

The introduction to this chapter provides a well-researched history of protest in the United States from the turn of the century through 1930. W. E. B. Du Bois's and Marcus Garvey's impact on the period are discussed. The chapter, itself, includes writings of Du Bois, Langston Hughes, A. Philip Randolph, and Garvey. Among topics discussed are the Niagara Movement, Garvey's philosophies, and Hughes's involvement with the National Association for the Advancement of Colored People (NAACP). There is an extensive bibliography and an index. Grant's commentary is intelligent and objective. Written for those interested in African American studies, it is equally useful for grades 7 through 12 and above.

Harris, Gloria A. "The 135th Street Library." **Cobblestone** 12, no. 2 (February 1991): 28–30.

The 135th Street Library was very active during the Harlem Renaissance. An afternoon at the library might include storytime with Langston Hughes, a visit by Countee Cullen and his students, or a contest sponsored by Jessie Fauset. Those activities are detailed in this brief article, which also includes the reminiscences of a former librarian and several black-and-white photographs. *Cobblestone* is written for students in grades 4 through 9, but much of the information in this issue, devoted entirely to the Harlem Renaissance, is not found elsewhere. Single copies are available from the publisher for $4.50.

Haskins, Jim. **The Harlem Renaissance**. Brookfield, CT: Millbrook Press, 1996. 192p. $21.90. ISBN 1-56294-565-3.

Haskins's arrangement of this work is by theme. In Chapter 1, Haskins discusses the Harlem Renaissance as a process. Chapter 2 provides a discussion of Harlem, itself, and remaining chapters cover specific fields of endeavor: music, dance, musical theatre, poetry and fiction, and painters and sculptors. Haskins's historical analysis of Harlem is well done. Topics include the effect of the Great Migration on Harlem. Marcus Garvey, W. E. B. Du Bois, and Alain Locke are discussed. Haskins profiles Bill Robinson, Ethel Waters, and Duke Ellington, among others. Also included are excerpts of writing by Harlem Renaissance notables. A selection from *His Eye Is on the Sparrow*, Ethel Waters's biography, tells of her meeting with Carl Van Vechten. Writer Rudolph Fischer describes how Harlem nightclubs changed as a result of White clientele flocking to uptown clubs. Along with his biographical sketches, Haskins provides information on the Harmon Foundation, which awarded prizes to writers and artists of the era. Curiously, Haskins makes no mention of Nella Larsen, Fats Waller, Fletcher Henderson, or Louis Armstrong, all of whom were important figures during the Harlem Renaissance. The work contains two bibliographies: one for adults and one for students in grades 7 through 12. This book is recommended for both audiences.

Hornsby, Alton, Jr. **Chronology of African-American History: Significant Events and People from 1619 to the Present**. Detroit, MI: Gale Research, 1991. 570p. $60.00. ISBN 0-8103-7093-X.

Hornsby's lengthy introduction provides an overview of each period of African American history. Of interest to those researching the Harlem Renaissance will be chapter 5, which deals with the years 1918–32. Arranged in chronological order, day by day, the book focuses on events and people. Included are illustrations for each period. Hornsby's work provides good background on the climate of the 1920s in Harlem, and the day-by-day arrangement makes this source unique. Although not comprehensive, this is a good reference for social history. It is appropriate for grades 7 through 12 and above.

Kellner, Bruce, ed. **The Harlem Renaissance: A Historical Dictionary of the Era**. Westport, CT: Greenwood, 1984. 476p. $65.00. ISBN 0-313-23232-6.

A dictionary format is used to cover several aspects of the Harlem Renaissance. Signed entries include information on people, literary works, periodicals, films, music, art, and politics. A chronology details significant events, and a glossary defines Harlem slang. The book also includes excellent coverage of lesser-known aspects of the time. Written for adults and researchers, the book is appropriate for grades 7 through 12 as well.

Lewis, David Levering. **When Harlem Was in Vogue**. New York: Oxford University Press, 1981. 400p. $13.95. ISBN 0-19-505969-7.

Lewis is an established expert in his field. He covers every aspect of the Harlem Renaissance, from major movements, such as Garveyism to fads, from literary salons to cabarets, and from major writers and artists to lesser-known figures. Featured are several black-and-white photographs. The chapter "Enter the New Negro" discusses at length the factors that brought about the Harlem Renaissance. This thoroughly researched book is full of anecdotes, reminiscences, and interesting facts. Written in narrative form, chapters proceed in chronological order. Index is by name and subject. Lewis's book, recommended in *The Senior High School Catalog*, and by *Library Journal*, is an excellent source for grades 7 through 12 and above.

Low, W. Augustus, ed., and Virgil A. Clift, assoc. ed. "Harlem." In **Encyclopedia of Black America**. Quality Paperbacks Series. New York: Da Capo, 1984. Reprint. 941p. $35.00. ISBN 0-306-80221-X.

Although this entire volume is well worth looking at, the lengthy section on Harlem is especially informative. The entry opens with a photograph of a street scene near the Apollo Theatre during the early 1930s. The article is rich in detail about the history of Harlem, its geographical location, and how Harlem changed from a White suburban enclave into an African American community. The encyclopedia format makes this book easily accessible for grades 7 through 12 and above.

Meltzer, Milton, ed. **The Black Americans: A History in Their Own Words, 1619–1983**. Rev. ed. New York: Crowell, 1984. 320p. $15.89. ISBN 0-690-04418-6.

Meltzer has collected a variety of letters, speeches, documents, and eyewitness accounts of the history of Black people in the United States. A section on the 1920s and 1930s features reproductions of original material. Meltzer discusses Marcus Garvey, W. E. B. Du Bois, and A. Philip Randolph, and makes reference to the Harlem Renaissance. Meltzer is a highly regarded, award-winning writer. His works are usually geared to young adult readers, but this is appropriate for grades 10 through 12.

Osofsky, Gilbert. **Harlem: The Making of a Ghetto, Negro New York: 1890–1930**. New York: Harper Torch Books, 1971. 276p. ISBN 06-131572-9.

Although out of print at this time, Osofsky's work is worth examining as it is a social history of Harlem, itself. The author traces Harlem's evolution from a pristine suburb to its decline during the Great Depression of the 1930s. Osofsky examines the effects of the Great Migration, alienation, racism, and the New Negro Movement on Harlem. The author's discussion of the Harlem Renaissance includes an examination of its shortcomings. Osofsky's research is based on an examination of periodicals, newspapers, census reports, and municipal documents of the era. The result of Osofsky's work is a true picture of life in Harlem, which contrasts sharply with the glamorous, exotic nightlife enjoyed by those who went uptown for a night of revelry. In the light of day, life in Harlem was harsh for many of its residents.

Part 3 of this work focuses on the Harlem Renaissance, but the entire book provides a historical background, enabling readers to understand the why and how of Harlem as it was. Included are black-and-white photographs and a bibliographical essay. Recommended for grades 7 through 12 and above.

Richardson, Janine. "Opportunity Knocks." **Cobblestone** 12, no. 2. (February 1991): 6–9.

Although this article is brief, it provides an excellent account of March 21, 1924, the day a number of White publishers, editors, and writers met with a group of young African American writers at a Civic Club dinner. The article discusses the dinner and the foundations, organizations, and businesses that made financial contributions to the writers and artists at the dinner. Several black-and-white photographs are included. Written for students in grades 4 through 9, this article provides information not found elsewhere.

Salzman, Jack et al. **Encyclopedia of African American Culture and History**. 5 vols. New York: Macmillan, 1996. $425.00. ISBN 0-02-897345-3.

Beginning with the arrival of slaves and ending in the present day, this set surveys achievements and issues of African Americans. Many Harlem Renaissance notables are discussed, including Marcus Garvey and Langston Hughes, with entries written by their biographers. Included are bibliographies for each entry and more than 1,000 black-and-white photographs. "Pulitzer

Prize Winners" is only one of several appendixes. Salzman presents a thorough coverage of African American history. Written in encyclopedic form, it is excellent for research or browsing. Recommended for grades 7 through 12 and above.

Schoener, Allon, ed. **Harlem on My Mind: Cultural Capital of Black America 1900–1968**. With an introduction by Candice Van Ellison. New York: New Press, 1995. 272p. $19.95. ISBN 1-56584-266-9.

Originally an exhibition at the Metropolitan Museum of Art, this work is actually a collection of newspaper articles arranged chronologically. The 1920–29 section consists of reportage from several newspapers of the day, covering such topics as Marcus Garvey, the Great Migration, James Weldon Johnson's views on Anglo-Saxons, the New Negro, and the dance craze created by the Charleston. Candice Van Ellison's introduction provides information on the history of Harlem, as well as a discussion of issues, such as housing, education, and employment. This is a fascinating collection of articles on a wide variety of topics. Also included are several photographs covering all aspects of life in Harlem. Recommended for grades 7 through 12 and above.

Smith, Jessie Carney. **Images of Blacks in American Culture: A Reference Guide to Information Sources**. Westport, CT: Greenwood, 1988. 384p. $65.00. ISBN 0-313-24844-3.

Smith, a librarian, discusses imagery in the literature, theatre, music, film, and art of African Americans. Among the many references are those of Harlem Renaissance writers and artists. Smith even presents a discussion of toys and games. Each essay concludes with a bibliography. Smith's work is included here because it is an excellent source of information not found elsewhere. Furthermore, it is an excellent starting point for research. Written for adults, it is also recommended for grades 7 through 12.

Smith, Jessie Carney, ed. with Caspar Jordan and Robert L. Johns. **Black Firsts: 2,000 Years of Extraordinary Achievement**. Detroit, MI: Visible Ink, 1994. 529p. $16.95. ISBN 0-8103-9490-1.

Smith has published several books on African American culture. This is another example of her award-winning work. Several features make this an exceptional resource: a fold-out time line, a month-by-month calendar of "firsts," and an index by year. The index by year is especially helpful for zeroing in on firsts during the Harlem Renaissance. More firsts occurred during the 1920s than any prior decade. The book is arranged by field of endeavor. Thus, the table of contents allows readers to locate information from many fields, including "Arts and Entertainment," "Civil Rights," "Government," "Journalism," "Sports," and "Writers." Firsts in each field are arranged chronologically. Details of the achievement are provided as well as the source from which the attribution comes, with page numbers. This informative and fun-to-browse resource is recommended for grades 7 through 12 and above.

Stewart, Jeffrey C. **1001 Things Everyone Should Know About African American History**. New York: Doubleday, 1996. 406p. $22.46. ISBN 0-385-47309-5.

Two of Stewart's intended purposes for this work are to serve as a basic text for anyone who has limited knowledge of African American history and as a textbook supplement for high school students. The work has a textbook look, the language is clear and straightforward, making it an excellent source. The book is organized by theme, with information for each theme arranged chronologically. An extensive section covers the Harlem Renaissance. After a brief introduction, Stewart summarizes "Some Important Books." Also included are biographical sketches and several black-and-white photographs. Because of the book's thematic organization, the index must be used to access information on such African American notables as W. E. B. Du Bois, Paul Robeson, and Walter White, who are all discussed in a section called "Civil Rights and Politics." Stewart covers a vast amount of material and provides information not found in other sources. The book is both informative and fun to browse. Recommended for grades 7 through 12 and above.

Watson, Steven. **The Harlem Renaissance: Hub of African American Culture, 1920–1930**. Circles of 20th Century Series. New York: Pantheon Books, 1995. 224p. $22.00. ISBN 0-679-42370-2.

This fascinating collection of information on the Harlem Renaissance covers just about everything the student researcher would want to know about the period. There are maps, definitions, and quotations, in addition to many black-and-white photographs. Watson demonstrates a thorough knowledge of his subject and has created not only an informative but a fun-to-browse book that is hard to put down. He has even included a diagram explaining the professional and personal relationships of Harlem Renaissance writers. An excellent chronology and a nonfiction bibliography round out the book. Highly recommended for grades 7 through 12 and above.

William Greaves Productions, prod. **From These Roots**. New York: William Greaves Productions in Association with The Schomburg Center for Research in Black Culture. Videocassette, 29 minutes.

Narrated by actor Brock Peters, this film examines themes and forces in the Harlem Renaissance. It touches on all aspects of the Harlem Renaissance; artists, writers, actors, entertainers, and scholars are discussed. Poetry by Langston Hughes, Claude McKay, and Countee Cullen is read by Peters. Black-and-white photos, music, and the narration blend perfectly to present an overview of the movement and of Harlem. Produced for students, this film is an excellent introduction to the era. Recommended for grades 7 through 12.

Cultural and Biographical References

The references listed here contain information either on several topics or on several individuals discussed in the various categories used in this work. They are excellent sources, and because of the wide variety of information they offer, many of these references are good starting points for research. Kellner's and Lewis's works are excellent sources of information on all aspects of the Harlem Renaissance. Anderson's work traces the history of Harlem over a broader period of time. Other works are more general, but each provides a variety of information about one or more aspects of the Harlem Renaissance or about those who were actively involved in it. Not all references listed here present a historical perspective, nor is their coverage of the topic limited to a historical perspective. (See also chapter 1, "Historical Overview.")

Bibliography

Anderson, Jervis. **This Was Harlem: A Cultural Portrait, 1900–1950**. New York: Farrar, Straus & Giroux, 1982. 400p. $17.00. ISBN 0-374-27623-4.

Anderson presents a comprehensive study of Harlem, discussing social, political, and economic aspects of the community. Each topic is divided into chapters; for example, chapter 4 includes a thorough discussion of writers. Not only does Anderson provide details of the writers' works, he also discusses literary salons and patronage. Additionally, Anderson provides the same detail in discussing other aspects, such as Garveyism, W. E. B. Du Bois's impact on the era, and A. Philip Randolph's labor movement. Recommended for grades 10 through 12 and above.

Kellner, Bruce, ed. **The Harlem Renaissance: A Historical Dictionary of the Era**. Westport, CT: Greenwood, 1984. 476p. $65.00. ISBN 0-313-23232-6.

Kellner uses a dictionary format to cover events, places, people, literary works, drama, politics, film, and art. Most letters of the alphabet have several entries. Articles are signed by contributors, all of whom are experts in their field. The book also includes appendixes, such as a chronology of events and even a glossary of Harlem slang at the time of the Harlem Renaissance. There is excellent coverage of both the well-known and the lesser-known aspects of the Renaissance. Written in clear, straightforward language, this book is appropriate for those in grades 7 through 12 and above who are interested in the period.

Kranz, Rachel. **The Biographical Dictionary of Black Americans**. New York: Facts on File, 1991. 192p. $24.95. ISBN 0-8160-2324-7.

This book contains close to 200 short sketches on African Americans from all walks of life from Colonial days to the present. Among these are several famous names from the Harlem Renaissance. The book includes further sources for reading that are especially suited to young adults. Each entry reviews significant accomplishments, prizes, awards, and personal data. Also featured are several black-and-white photographs. Kranz wrote this book especially for students in grades 7 through 12.

Lee, George L. **Inspiring African Americans: Black History Makers in the United States, 1750–1984**. Jefferson, NC: McFarland, 1991. 144p. $18.95. ISBN 0-89950-576-7.

Lee, a talented caricaturist, has compiled a selection of portraits originally featured in his newspaper column, "Interesting People." Featured are African Americans from all walks of life: religion, sports, politics, entertainment, and the arts. The book includes both well-known and lesser-known individuals. Each portrait is skillfully drawn and includes a short biographical sketch. Lee's intent was not for this book to serve as a reference tool, but to inspire young people. Among the Harlem Renaissance personalities included are Langston Hughes, Zora Neale Hurston, Paul Robeson, and W. E. B. Du Bois. The layout is appealing, and the book should be useful to students in grades 7 through 10, for whom it was written.

Lewis, David Levering. **When Harlem Was in Vogue**. New York: Alfred A. Knopf, 1981. 400p. $13.95. ISBN 0-19-505969-7.

Lewis's work is a comprehensive narrative of the people and events that shaped the Harlem Renaissance. Moreover, it is a history of Harlem, itself. To a limited extent, chapters follow in chronological order. Each focuses on a different aspect of the era. Sprinkled throughout are anecdotes and reminiscences of meetings, parties, and literary and political gatherings. Lewis has thoroughly researched his work; he includes the street-corner politicians and neighborhood characters along with the famous. Lewis is a well-respected writer in the field of African American studies, and this book is one of the most popular written about the era. Intended for adults, it is also highly recommended for students in grades 7 through 12.

Low, W. Augustus, ed., and Virgil A. Clift, assoc. ed. **Encyclopedia of Black America**. Quality Paperback Series. New York: Da Capo, 1984. 941p. $35.00. ISBN 0-306-80221-X.

More than 1,400 biographical entries and approximately 125 topical articles make up Low and Clift's book. Also included are many black-and-white illustrations. Topical articles cover many areas of African American history and culture. Entries, including those related to the Harlem Renaissance, are divided into three types: articles, biographies, and cross-references. Many entries also contain bibliographical references. This is an outstanding reference tool and one of the most comprehensive available. In particular, the easy-to-use format makes it appropriate for grades 7 through 12.

Nagel, Carol DeKane, ed. **African American Reference Library**. Detroit, MI: Gale Research, 1994. 9 vols. $195.00. ISBN 0-8103-9230-5.

This comprehensive, nine-volume reference work consists of three separate sections: "African American Almanac," "African American Biography," and "African American Chronology." A black-and-white photograph accompanies each entry in the biography section. Each entry also features a quotation. The almanac section covers historical and cultural topics, with many references to the Harlem Renaissance. The chronology adds a historical perspective and explores milestones in African American history. The years of the Harlem Renaissance are well represented in this section. Written for grades 7 through 12.

Newman, Richard, comp. **Black Access: A Bibliography of Afro-American Bibliographies**. Westport, CT.: Greenwood, 1984. 249p. $49.95. ISBN 0-313-23282-2.

Newman hoped to find 500 articles for his work. Instead, he found more than 3,000 and thus had to limit coverage to African American and Canadian bibliographies. This bibliography contains books, articles, indexes, catalogs, guides, calendars, and checklists. Entries are not annotated, but a chronological index and a detailed subject index provide easy access to information for anyone researching the Harlem Renaissance. Designed for researchers interested in African American studies, the easy access makes it suitable for researchers in grades 10 through 12 as well.

Salley, Columbus. **The Black 100: A Ranking of the Most Influential African Americans, Past and Present**. New York: Citadel Press, 1993. 383p. $19.95. ISBN 0-8065-1299-7.

Salley's idea of ranking his subjects is thought provoking and should generate discussion of his rankings among readers. He provides biographical sketches of each, along with a black-and-white photograph and at least one quotation by or about the subject. Sketches include personal information and professional accomplishments. Of interest to Harlem Renaissance researchers are the sketches on W. E. B. Du Bois, Marcus Garvey, Paul Robeson, Walter White, Duke Ellington, Oscar Micheaux, and Marian Anderson. Appropriate for grades 7 through 12 and above.

Smith, Jessie Carney, ed. **Images of Blacks in American Culture: A Reference Guide to Information Sources**. Westport, CT: Greenwood, 1988. 384p. $65.00. ISBN 0-313-24844-3.

Smith, a librarian, discusses imagery in the literature, theatre, music, film, and art of African Americans. Smith has written several works on the Black experience and is well respected. For this work, she has gathered 10 specialists in the field. Their names will also be recognized by anyone using this guide. Many references include the works of Harlem Renaissance writers and artists, such as Langston Hughes, Countee Cullen, and Paul Robeson. Entries include essays on the subject, followed by excellent bibliographies. There is even a discussion of toys and games. This work is exceptional because the essays present a historical or sociological perspective. It is unique in that its subject matter is images. The work, written for researchers of Black studies, is suitable for grades 7 through 12 and above.

Stevenson, Rosemary M., comp. **Index to Afro-American Reference Sources**. Westport, CT: Greenwood, 1988. 344p. $74.95. ISBN 0-313-24580-0.

Stevenson has compiled an extensive list of reference sources of all kinds, including dictionaries, encyclopedias, bibliographies, and texts on the African American experience. Approximately 181 sources are cited. The book is easily accessible, thanks to author and title indexes. Using these, one can easily find references to sources dealing with the Harlem Renaissance and those who participated in it. It is a good starting point for further research. Easy access makes it suitable for researchers in grades 7 through 12 and above.

Watson, Steven. **The Harlem Renaissance: Hub of African American Culture, 1920–1930**. Circles of 20th Century Series. New York: Pantheon Books, 1995. $22.00. ISBN 0-679-42370-2.

Watson's work contains a wide variety of information pertaining to the Harlem Renaissance: maps, pictures, quotations, and definitions; there is even a diagram explaining the relationships between and among the writers of the era. Also featured are a chronology from 1920 to 1930 and a nonfiction bibliography. This is all in addition to the text, which is clearly written. Although Watson's book is a valuable reference tool, it is fun to browse as well. Recommended for grades 9 through 12 and above.

Williams, Michael W., ed. **The African American Encyclopedia**. North Bellmore, NY: Marshall Cavendish, 1993. 6 vols. 1,818p. $449.95. ISBN 1-85435-545-7.

Entries are arranged alphabetically, and coverage includes people, institutions, literary works, films, plays, musical groups, sports, places, and movements. Movements include those of Marcus Garvey and the Harlem Renaissance. In addition, many lesser-known individuals are included. This book is very well written and easy to read, making it a valuable reference tool for any library. It is an excellent choice for grades 7 through 12 and above.

PART II

Notable Contributors

Fig. 3.1.
Walter White (Schomburg Center, NYPL).

Major Influences

Among those African Americans who exerted a major influence on artistic aspects of the Harlem Renaissance were Charles S. Johnson, Jessie Fauset, Carl Van Vechten, Walter White, and Alain Locke. Each was an author who had works published during the Harlem Renaissance; however, each was also extremely influential in some aspect of the development of the Harlem Renaissance. They are listed here because their efforts in some way made the Harlem Renaissance possible. (See also part 3, "Literature and Writing," for information on their literary careers.) The works listed here highlight the influence each had on the movement.

Jessie Fauset

Jessie Fauset, herself a writer (see also chapter 6, "Literature"), edited *The Crisis*, the official publication of the National Association for the Advancement of Colored People (NAACP). In this capacity, she worked closely with W. E. B. Du Bois. Although she is more widely known as a novelist, she excelled as an editor: She was largely responsible for discovering the talents of many Harlem Renaissance writers, including Langston Hughes, Countee Cullen, and Jean Toomer. Fauset was also responsible for *The Brownie's Book*, a magazine for children that was published during the Harlem Renaissance.

Charles S. Johnson

Charles S. Johnson moved to New York in 1921, where he worked for the Urban League and edited *Opportunity*, the League's official publication. Among the articles he edited were those submitted by Langston Hughes, Claude McKay, and Countee Cullen. It was Johnson who instituted prizes given by the magazine for outstanding artistic achievement by African Americans. These prizes not only brought wide recognition to artists and writers but also provided encouragement to the African American artistic community.

The Civic Club dinner of March 21, 1924, brought together several aspiring African American writers and representatives of large publishing houses, critics, and intellectuals. The dinner was a huge success; publishers and critics were not only receptive, they were eager to publish the works of the young authors. It was Charles S. Johnson who organized this important event.

Alain Locke

Alain Locke was Harvard educated, one of the first recipients and the first African American recipient of a Rhodes scholarship, which enabled him to study at Oxford University in England. In 1925, Locke published *The New Negro: An Interpretation*, an anthology of works by African American writers, many of whom were associated with the Harlem Renaissance. This work introduced Americans to the Harlem Renaissance and to African American intellectualism.

Locke received financial support from Charlotte Mason, who would later, at Locke's recommendation, become patron to Langston Hughes and Zora Neale Hurston. He has been called the spokesperson of the Harlem Renaissance, as well as one of its architects.

Each of the sources below contains information about these major players who contributed to the development of the Harlem Renaissance.

Carl Van Vechten

Carl Van Vechten's impact on the Harlem Renaissance could be seen in two ways: He had influence, and he had flamboyance. Author of the controversial novel *Nigger Heaven*, he was fascinated by Harlem and by African Americans. As music editor of *Vanity Fair*, he had the ability to draw attention and recognition from the White literary world to Harlem. He also had many powerful connections in the publishing world and used them for the benefit of writers of the Harlem Renaissance.

Van Vechten's own flamboyance also made news; his escapades in Harlem with White celebrities were widely known, as were his lavish parties. This may not have been the type of attention desired by the intellectuals, many of whom thought he was a sensationalist. Nevertheless, Van Vechten made Harlem visible to White America. A talented writer, critic, and photographer, Van Vechten photographed many of his African American contemporaries. (See also chapter 11, "Photography.")

Van Vechten left behind an extensive collection of photos, writing, and memorabilia, which is now archived in collections in several libraries, including Yale University's library and the New York Public Library.

Walter White

Walter White was noted for his role in the National Association for the Advancement of Colored People (NAACP). It was he who helped the NAACP increase its membership through his powerful connections in the literary world. He worked tirelessly to promote the Harlem Renaissance, and his efforts were usually extremely successful. His appearance—blond hair and blue eyes—enabled him to pass for White, but he chose to do so only as a field representative for NAACP, a position in which he often infiltrated groups, like the Ku Klux Klan. He wrote three books: Two dealt with lynching, and one dealt with passing as a White person.

Bibliography

Fraser, Jane. **Walter White: Civil Rights Leader**. Black Americans of Achievement Series. New York: Chelsea House, 1990. 112p. $17.95. ISBN 1-55546-617-6.
Fraser's biography opens dramatically with an incident in Tennessee. A stranger in a small town, White converses with local men who brag to him about a lynching. White, fair-haired and blue-eyed, had to suppress not only his feelings but his identity. White was a African American and a field secretary for the National Association for the Advancement of Colored People (NAACP).
White was a fascinating man, and Fraser captures the true essence of his personality. She also provides details of his relationship with James Weldon Johnson, White's mentor in the organization, as well as his friend. White also published two novels during the Harlem Renaissance, *Flight* and *The Fire in the Flint*. Fraser discusses the influence of H. L. Mencken on White's literary efforts. Included are several black-and-white photographs, a chronology of White's achievements, and a bibliography. This well-researched book was written specifically for grades 7 through 9.

Kellner, Bruce, ed. **The Harlem Renaissance: A Historical Dictionary of the Era**. Westport, CT: Greenwood, 1984. 476p. $65.00. ISBN 0-313-23232-6.
Kellner's work, arranged alphabetically, is thoroughly researched and contains more information on aspects of the Harlem Renaissance than perhaps any other work. Kellner provides information on each of the major influences discussed in this chapter. His work is written for adults, but it is appropriate for grades 7 through 12 as well.

————. **"Keep A-Inchin' Along": Selected Writings of Carl Van Vechten About Black Arts and Letters**. Contributions in Afro-American and African Studies, No. 45. Westport, CT: Greenwood, 1979. 303p. ISBN 0-313-21091-8.
Kellner has compiled a wealth of information by and about Carl Van Vechten. Included are several pieces written by Van Vechten as critic; a belated introduction and prologue to his controversial novel, *Nigger Heaven*, and a section devoted to Van Vechten's best friend, James Weldon Johnson. The section "Portrait Memoirs" includes Van Vechten's personal reminiscences of his contemporaries, many of whom were associated with the

Harlem Renaissance. Kellner has included several black-and-white photographs taken by Van Vechten and a selection of his correspondence, which spans a period of 40 years; Van Vechten most often wrote to Walter White, James Weldon Johnson, and Langston Hughes. In his introduction Kellner discusses at length Van Vechten's role in the Harlem Renaissance and his possible motives for such involvement. Kellner has compiled an excellent selection of materials. Written for adults, this work is also appropriate for grades 10 through 12.

Kishimoto, Hisao. **Carl Van Vechten: The Man and His Role in the Harlem Renaissance**. Tokyo: Seibodo, 1983. 148p.

Kishimoto's work opens with black-and-white photographs of and by Carl Van Vechten. Included are details of Van Vechten's childhood, his fascination with African Americans, and his influence on the Harlem Renaissance. Kishimoto also discusses Van Vechten's impact on race relations in America. The work is insightful, and the reader gains knowledge of the personal side of Van Vechten. Appendixes include a chronology of Van Vechten's life and a list of famous African Americans with whom he was associated. Written for adults, this work is also appropriate for students in grades 10 through 12.

Kranz, Rachel. **The Biographical Dictionary of Black Americans**. New York: Facts on File, 1991. 192p. $24.95. ISBN 0-8160-2324-7.

Kranz has compiled nearly 200 biographical sketches of African Americans from all fields of endeavor, including those of Alain Locke, Jessie Fauset, Charles S. Johnson, and Walter White. Entries detail significant accomplishments, prizes, awards, and personal data. Many black-and-white photographs are included. Written for grades 7 through 10.

Lueders, Edward. **Carl Van Vechten**. New York: Twayne, 1965. 158p. $13.95. ISBN 0-80840-070-3.

Lueders focuses on Van Vechten's professional life, making this a good companion resource to Kishimoto's book. Van Vechten's works written before, during, and after the Harlem Renaissance are summarized and analyzed by Lueders. Although Lueders provides few details on Van Vechten's personal life, he discusses thoroughly Van Vechten's career as critic, writer, and photographer. Lueders presents Van Vechten as a man who was immensely talented and passionate about his work and about the Harlem Renaissance. Written for adults, this book is also appropriate for grades 10 through 12.

Richardson, Janine. "Opportunity Knocks." **Cobblestone** 12, no. 2 (February 1991): 6–9.

Although this article is brief, it details the Civic Club dinner organized by Charles S. Johnson on March 21, 1924. This dinner became a turning point of the Harlem Renaissance, as the publishing world subsequently opened up to young African American writers. Several black-and-white photographs and illustrations are included, along with listings of the organizations, foundations, and businesses that contributed to the Harlem Renaissance. Written for students in grades 4 through 9, the article contains information not found elsewhere.

Sylvander, Carolyn Wedin. **Jessie Redmon Fauset, Black American Writer**. Troy, NY: Whitston Publishing, 1981. 276p. $18.50. SBN 0-87875-196-3.

Sylvander's work offers more than biographical information on Jessie Fauset. According to the author, Fauset's work is often unfairly maligned. Thus, she traces Fauset's life in an effort to explain and defend Fauset's writing. The premise is that the details of Fauset's personal life reveal not only her character but also her struggles against sexism and racism, thus providing a parallel between the strengths and weaknesses of Fauset's character and those of her writing. In the section on Fauset's life from 1919 to 1961, Sylvander discusses Fauset's editorial work at *The Crisis* and her relationship with W. E. B. Du Bois. Details of Fauset's day-to-day activities as editor of the periodical are included here, clearly illustrating that Fauset was an influential woman of the Harlem Renaissance. Written for adults, this book is also appropriate for grades 10 through 12.

Waldron, Edward E. **Walter White and the Harlem Renaissance**. Port Washington, NY: Kennikat Press, 1978. 186p. ISBN 0-8046-9197-5.

Walter White is usually noted for his association with the National Association for the Advancement of Colored People (NAACP) and for his novels published during the Harlem Renaissance. However, White was also an important major force in the development of the Harlem Renaissance. Of particular interest in this work is chapter 2, "The Harlem Renaissance: A Time for Opportunities," in which Waldron presents a picture of the social climate of the era. Harlem's middle class, relationships between the community and artists, and the issue of race in literature are all discussed thoughtfully.

Although the bulk of this work is devoted to White's novels, chapter 5, "Literary Counselor and Friend," presents White in the role of major influencer. He was powerful, had many contacts, and never hesitated to use his contacts to help others. This is an excellent source of information on White that cannot be found elsewhere. Written for adults, it is also appropriate for grades 10 through 12.

Fig. 4.1.
Marcus Garvey's wedding photograph, taken Christmas, 1919,
on the occasion of his wedding to Amy Ashwood,
the first Mrs. Garvey and co-founder of the
Universal Negro Improvement Association (UNIA)
in Jamaica, 1914 (Schomburg Center, NYPL).

Political Activists

Several people active during the Harlem Renaissance demonstrated extraordinary leadership qualities. Each had a tremendous impact on the movement. They were active in various and often conflicting fields of endeavor, yet they all had the same sense of purpose: overcoming inequality. They are W. E. B. Du Bois, scholar, author, and editor; Marcus Garvey, prominent Black nationalist; James Weldon Johnson, author, composer, and diplomat; Walter White, author and activist; and A. Philip Randolph, labor organizer.

W. E. B. Du Bois

W. E. B. Du Bois, a Harvard-educated scholar, was truly an intellectual. His work reflects not only his excellent education but also his passion for people. He worked tirelessly for equality and recognition for African Americans. As editor of *The Crisis*, the official magazine of the National Association for the Advancement of Colored People (NAACP), he was instrumental in publishing the works of young writers. Considered to be elitist by some, he denounced Marcus Garvey and thought that jazz and nightclubs were not only demeaning to African American culture but also responsible for perpetuating negative stereotypes of African Americans. He believed America needed to be exposed to Black intellectualism to destroy old stereotypes.

Marcus Garvey

Marcus Garvey, born in Jamaica, moved to Harlem in 1916 and began his movement by talking to passersby on Harlem street corners. His word spread quickly, and soon the Universal Negro Improvement Association (UNIA) was formed. Garvey believed that Blacks could not succeed in a White world. His "Back to Africa" movement would enable all Africans to return to Africa and prosper. Garvey's power was short-lived. In the mid-1920s he was convicted of mail fraud and sentenced to prison. He was eventually released and deported to Jamaica. He had many followers and published *The Negro Weekly*, the official newspaper of the UNIA.

25

James Weldon Johnson

James Weldon Johnson was born in Florida and eventually became principal of the elementary school he attended as a child. He left Florida for New York after successfully composing and presenting an opera in his home state. Johnson and his brother, John Rosamond Johnson, wrote "Lift Every Voice and Sing," which was to become an anthem for African Americans. He also wrote poetry and musical compositions in the 1920s. He was a driving force in the National Association for the Advancement of Colored People (NAACP) during the Harlem Renaissance.

A. Philip Randolph

A. Philip Randolph moved to New York City as part of the Great Migration. Determined to fight racism, Randolph studied socialism and public speaking at City College. He soon became well known on the streets of Harlem, where he put forth his radical ideas. He championed equal rights for Black Pullman porters in the labor movement and organized the Brotherhood of Sleeping Car Porters in 1925. As editor of *The Messenger*, the radical monthly magazine founded by Randolph and Owen Chandler, he wrote strong editorials denouncing unfair labor policies.

Walter White

Walter White was a major force in the Harlem Renaissance. He authored two books during the Harlem Renaissance: *Flight* and *The Fire in the Flint*. As field secretary for the National Association for the Advancement of Colored People (NAACP) in the South, White investigated lynchings. White was so effective that James Weldon Johnson brought him to New York. In addition to his work for the NAACP, White worked tirelessly to bring attention and recognition to writers and artists. He seemed to know every important person in New York. He used his connections whenever he could, and his efforts enabled many to attain recognition.

Each of these men had his own answers for overcoming the injustice and prejudice that African Americans faced. They may not have agreed with each other's solutions, but they all made a significant contribution to the Black struggle for civil rights, which was an important component of the Harlem Renaissance.

Learn more about these men by reading the following books.

Bibliography

Cronon, E. David. **Black Moses: The Story of Marcus Garvey and the Universal Negro Improvement Association**. Madison: University of Wisconsin Press, 1969. 278p. $12.95. ISBN 0-299-01214-X.

Cronon's work is thoroughly researched and written from a different perspective than that of Tony Martin, whose works on Garvey and UNIA have a political point of view. When Cronon began his research, Garvey had all but disappeared into obscurity. The author believed that Garvey, more than any other individual, was responsible for racial pride among African Americans. This may be disputed by some, but Cronon's work covers all aspects of Garvey's life in great detail. A major portion of the work focuses on Garvey's activities during the 1920s. Recommended for grades 7 through 12 and above.

Estell, Kenneth, ed. "Black Nationalism." In **Reference Library of Black America**. 5 vols. Detroit, MI: Gale Research, 1993. 1,600p. $179.90. ISBN 0-685-49222-2.

This chapter presents a thorough, chronological background of Black nationalist movements, as well as information on Marcus Garvey, one of the most widely known Black nationalists. Each volume is indexed, making this reference easy to use. It is also heavily illustrated. Access is through name and key word index. An extensive bibliography is broken down by topic. This set is written especially for students in grades 7 through 12.

Fraser, Jane. **Walter White: Civil Rights Leader**. Black Americans of Achievement Series. New York: Chelsea House, 1990. 112p. $17.95. ISBN 1-55546-617-6.

Fraser's biography opens dramatically with an incident in Tennessee. A stranger in a small town, White is engaged in conversation with locals who are bragging about their part in a lynching. White, fair-haired and blue-eyed, had to hide his identity. He was field secretary for the National Association for the Advancement of Colored People (NAACP). He was also an African American. As field secretary, he had to investigate lynchings; as a result, he often found himself in dangerous situations. Fraser captures the essence of this fascinating man. The biography includes details of his relationship with James Weldon Johnson, a close friend and employer. Fraser's book is clearly written and well researched. Rounding out the book are several black-and-white photographs, a chronology of achievements, and a bibliography. Written for grades 7 through 10.

Garvey, Amy Jacques. **Garvey and Garveyism**. New York: Macmillan, 1976. Reprint. 326p. ISBN 0-870-52351-1.

Written by Marcus Garvey's widow, this book details Garvey's life and political activities as a major force in Harlem during the Renaissance. Mrs. Garvey's account is rich in detail. There are no photographs, but excerpts of many original documents, letters, and speeches bring the period to life. The book includes many "inside" details that only someone close to Garvey would know. Garvey's United Negro Improvement Association (UNIA) involvement is also covered in depth. Although out of print, the book is included here because of the many excerpts it contains and because of Mrs. Garvey's input. This book is for adults, but is also appropriate for grades 10 through 12.

Grant, Joanne. "The 20th Century." In **Black Protest: History, Documents and Analyses, 1619 to the Present**. 2d ed. Black History Titles Series. New York: Fawcett Premier, 1991. 507p. $4.95. ISBN 0-449-30044-7.

The introduction to this chapter provides a well-researched history of protest in the United States from the turn of the century through 1930. W. E. B. Du Bois's and Marcus Garvey's influences on the Harlem Renaissance are discussed. The chapter, itself, includes writings of Du Bois, Langston Hughes, A. Philip Randolph, and Garvey. Among topics discussed are the Niagara Movement, Garvey's philosophies, and Hughes's involvement with the National Association for the Advancement of Colored People (NAACP).

This book features an extensive bibliography and an index. Grant's commentary is intelligent and objective. Written for those interested in African American studies, this book is equally useful for grades 7 through 12.

Hanley, Sally A. **A. Philip Randolph**. Black Americans of Achievement Series. New York: Chelsea House, 1989. 112p. $17.95. ISBN 1-55546-607-9.

A. Philip Randolph devoted his life to establishing fair working conditions for Blacks in America. In 1925, he organized a labor union, the Brotherhood of Sleeping Car Porters. The efforts of this tireless leader of the Black working man are recounted in this biography. Included are many black-and-white photographs and some reproductions of original documents, along with a reading list and a chronology of important events in Randolph's life. Written for grades 7 through 10.

Johnson, James Weldon. **Along This Way: The Autobiography of James Weldon Johnson**. American Biography Series. Temecula, CA: Reprint Services Corp., 1991. Reprint. 418p. $89.00. ISBN 0-7812-8221-7.

This book details the life of James Weldon Johnson, a truly extraordinary man. Written in 1933, the bulk of this work covers the period prior to the Harlem Renaissance. However, as an active member in the movement, Johnson's life is fascinating and inspiring. The final sections of the book are devoted to the years of the Harlem Renaissance. His writing is an honest and factual account of his association with various agencies, notably, the National Association for the Advancement of Colored People (NAACP). Johnson also provides details about the writing of his works. Recommended for grades 7 through 12 and above.

LaBlanc, Michael L., ed. **Contemporary Black Biography: Profiles from the International Black Community**. Detroit, MI: Gale Research, 1992. 525p. $45.00. ISBN 0-8103-8554-6.

The title of this volume might lead one to think that only living or contemporary personalities are profiled. This is not the case. Included are Harlem Renaissance personalities, one of which is Marcus Garvey. Garvey, discussed in detail, was selected, along with other Renaissance personalities, because of his continuing influence on African American culture. The treatment of subjects is sincere, and the text is well written. Entries are in alphabetical order. Indexes are by name, nationality, subject, and field of endeavor. The layout is attractive, and the photographs are excellent. This is an exceptional source for students in grades 7 through 12.

Lawlor, Mary. **Marcus Garvey: Black Nationalist Leader**. Black Americans of Achievement Series. New York: Chelsea House, 1988. 112p. $17.95. ISBN 1-55546-587-0.

This well-written biography tells of Garvey's childhood in Jamaica, his early interest in political activities, and his efforts to improve the status of Blacks in Jamaica. In 1916, he arrived in New York and, within three months, began lecturing and fund-raising. Lawlor provides in-depth coverage of these activities and Garvey's formation of the Universal Negro Improvement Association (UNIA). Also included are a bibliography, a chronology, and many black-and-white photographs of Garvey, UNIA parades, conventions, and worldwide activities. Finally, Lawlor discusses Garvey's impact on the Harlem Renaissance. Written for grades 7 through 10, this book is also a good source of information for adults.

Levy, Eugene. **James Weldon Johnson: Black Leader, Black Voice**. Negro Biographies and Autobiographies Series. Ann Arbor, MI: Books on Demand, 1973. 393p. $112.10. ISBN 0-8357-8927-6.

James Weldon Johnson was a successful high school principal, lawyer, librettist, writer, diplomat, civil rights leader, and university professor. That he accomplished all of this is noteworthy; that he accomplished it in a time when opportunities for African Americans were, at best, limited is extraordinary.

Levy has written a detailed account of Johnson's life. The work is thoroughly researched, making it one of the better biographies. Included are excellent accounts of Johnson's involvement with the National Association for the Advancement of Colored People (NAACP) and of his associations with W. E. B. Du Bois and Walter White. Levy also devotes an entire chapter to the Harlem Renaissance, focusing on Johnson's literary pursuits, his relationships with Langston Hughes and Claude McKay, and his life in Harlem. Excellent for its detail, for its coverage of the era, and for Levy's clear and factual narrative. Recommended for grades 7 through 12 and above.

Lewis, David Levering. **W. E. B. Du Bois: Biography of a Race**. New York: Henry Holt, 1993. 700p. $35.00. ISBN 0-8050-2621-5.

Lewis, a highly regarded scholar, presents an all-inclusive biography of W. E. B. Du Bois. Among Du Bois's many accomplishments detailed in this book is his founding of *The Crisis*, the official NAACP magazine that published the writing of many Harlem Renaissance authors. Included in Lewis's book are many historically significant photographs. This book is excellent for its thorough coverage of the political climate that led to the Harlem Renaissance. Written for adults, this volume is also appropriate for grades 7 through 12.

Pfeffer, Paula F. **A. Philip Randolph, Pioneer of the Civil Rights Movement**. Baton Rouge: Louisiana State University Press, 1990. 356p. $32.50. ISBN 0-8071-1554-1.

Much of Pfeffer's work is devoted to A. Philip Randolph's activities after the Harlem Renaissance; however, the material is relevant as Randolph was an active participant in the Harlem Renaissance. Pfeffer's opening chapters discuss the racial climate in America and the factors that led to Randolph's organization of sleeping car porters in 1925. In her preface, Pfeffer discusses Randolph's qualities as a leader and a man. Recommended for grades 7 through 12.

Stafford, Mark. **W. E. B. Du Bois: Scholar and Activist**. Black Americans of Achievement Series. New York: Chelsea House, 1989. 128p. $17.95. ISBN 1-55546-528-X.

This book traces W. E. B. Du Bois's career, his childhood, his education, and his relationships with other personalities of the Harlem Renaissance. Although there is less focus on his personal life, the biography is rich in detail of his activities and his impact on the Harlem Renaissance. There is a thorough discussion of the many publications he founded and edited. His role in the founding of the National Association for the Advancement of Colored People (NAACP) and his feud with Marcus Garvey are discussed in detail as well. Appendixes include a list of Du Bois's works, a chronology, and a bibliography. Includes many black-and-white photographs. Written for grades 7 through 10.

Tolbert-Rouchaleau, Jane. **James Weldon Johnson**. Black Americans of Achievement Series. New York: Chelsea House, 1988. 112p. $17.95. ISBN 1-55546-596-X.

James Weldon Johnson was a man of many talents: He composed music, served as a diplomat, and was politically active during the Harlem Renaissance. He became a chief executive of the National Association for the Advancement of Colored People (NAACP) during the Harlem Renaissance and significantly increased its membership, making it a powerful political force. All of these and other significant events in his life and career are detailed here. Included is a chronology and bibliography. There are also many excellent black-and-white photographs. Recommended for grades 7 through 10.

Vincent, Theodore, ed. **Voices of a Black Nation: Political Journalism in the Harlem Renaissance**. Trenton, NJ: Africa World, 1991. 391p. $35.00. ISBN 0-86543-202-3.

During the Harlem Renaissance, several African American weekly publications enjoyed large circulations. Vincent's collection of political commentary covers the years 1917–34, roughly the years of the Harlem Renaissance. A variety of political ideologies of the time are covered in this work. Several pieces allude to the feud between W. E. B. Du Bois and Marcus Garvey. Others discuss the "New Negro," a term adapted from Alain Locke's book to describe Black intellectuals. Also included are pieces by A. Philip Randolph and Du Bois. Vincent's work is a firsthand account of political and philosophical beliefs of the era. Recommended for grades 10 through 12 and adults.

Waldron, Edward E. **Walter White and the Harlem Renaissance**. Port Washington, NY: Kennikat Press, 1978. 186p. ISBN 0-8046-9197-5.

Walter White is usually known for his association with the National Association for the Advancement of Colored People (NAACP) and for his novels written during the Harlem Renaissance. White was a political activist until the day he died. His physical appearance would have enabled him to "pass" for White, but he never chose to do so unless it was in the course of doing undercover work for the NAACP. Waldron's chapter 2, "The Harlem Renaissance: A Time of Opportunities," presents a picture of the social climate of the times. Although the bulk of this work deals with White's literary talents, this is an important source on White as it contains information not found elsewhere. Recommended for grades 10 through 12 and above.

Weinberg, Meyer, ed. **The World of W. E. B. Du Bois: A Quotation Sourcebook**. Westport, CT: Greenwood, 1992. 282p. $65.00. ISBN 0-313-28619-1.

More than 1,000 quotations, all credited to W. E. B. Du Bois, are arranged by topic. There are 20 topics in all; each is its own chapter. Topics include "Education," "Racism," "Women," "Literature," and "White People." Each quotation is preceded by a title that provides a key to the content of the quotation. An index to quotations lists quotes by Du Bois by decade. This is an excellent source for anyone interested in Du Bois's views. Recommended for grades 7 through 12 and above.

Wright, Sarah E. **A. Philip Randolph: Integration in the Workplace**. The History of the Civil Rights Movement Series. Morristown, NJ: Silver Burdett, 1990. 130p. $7.95. ISBN 0-382-09922-2.

Written especially for young adults, this biography traces A. Philip Randolph's public and private life. Discussed are the influence of Booker T. Washington's passive philosophy, W. E. B. Du Bois's disagreement with it, and Randolph's own beginnings in politics. As a student at City College, Randolph met Chandler Owen, with whom he founded *The Messenger*. Wright devotes an entire chapter to *The Messenger*, as well as to Marcus Garvey, whom Randolph initially supported, and to the formation of the Brotherhood of Sleeping Car Porters. All of these events occurred during the Harlem Renaissance. Included are several black-and-white photographs, a "Civil Rights Movement Time Line," a "Timetable of Events in the Life of A. Philip Randolph," and a bibliography. Recommended for grades 7 through 10.

Fig. 5.1.
Jessie Fauset, painted by Laura Wheeler Waring
(Schomburg Center, NYPL).

Women of the Harlem Renaissance

While women have been profiled in other areas of this guide, those profiles and works related to them are listed in this section as well to assist those who wish to research women of the Harlem Renaissance.

The women of the Harlem Renaissance, many of whom are lesser known than their male counterparts, made many and varied contributions to the movement. Fortunately, recent research has led to recognition for many of these talented women.

Marian Anderson

Marian Anderson grew up in Philadelphia, where she sang in a church choir. Members of her church were so impressed with her abilities that they collected money so that she could study voice. Anderson had a brilliant career, but she had to overcome bigotry and initial failure as a concert singer. During the Harlem Renaissance, Anderson won a singing competition, which finally opened the door to success, first in Europe and later in the United States. Some years after the Renaissance, Anderson was still a victim of bigotry. The Daughters of the American Revolution prevented her from performing at Constitution Hall in Washington, D.C. On learning of this, First Lady Eleanor Roosevelt arranged to have Anderson sing on the steps of the Lincoln Memorial instead.

Josephine Baker

Josephine Baker was born in St. Louis, Missouri, and danced in vaudeville as a child. At the age of 15, she was in the chorus of *Shuffle Along*. She soon became a sensation on Broadway, but an offer to star in a revue in Paris changed the course of her life. Baker stayed in Paris and became a star of the Folies Bergère, a Parisian music hall known for its lavish and sometimes risqué productions. She was known for her dancing, especially her energetic performance of the Charleston and the

Black Bottom. In time she added singing to her act. Baker was truly charismatic. Her personal life is fascinating as well: During World War II, she was a spy for the French government, for which she was awarded the French Legion of Honor, the country's highest honor.

JESSIE FAUSET

Jessie Fauset, herself a writer, edited *The Crisis*, the official publication of the National Association for the Advancement of Colored People (NAACP). In this capacity, she worked closely with W. E. B. Du Bois. Although she is more widely known as a novelist, she excelled as an editor. She was largely responsible for discovering the talents of many Harlem Renaissance writers, including Langston Hughes, Countee Cullen, and Jean Toomer. Fauset was also responsible for *The Brownie's Book*, a magazine for children which was published during the Harlem Renaissance. Her novels include *There Is Confusion*, *Plum Bun*, and *The Chinaberry Tree*.

ALBERTA HUNTER

Alberta Hunter was one of the first women to record the blues. Her career began when she ran away from home and began singing for money. She was known for her rendition of "A Good Man Is Hard to Find" and also recorded "Down Hearted Blues," first made popular by Bessie Smith. Hunter successfully toured Europe and recorded several blues songs in the 1920s. She spent many years out of the limelight before returning to sing publicly in the late 1970s. She performed until her death in 1984.

ZORA NEALE HURSTON

Zora Neale Hurston was born in Florida in 1903. She studied at Howard University with Alain Locke, one of the major contributors to the Harlem Renaissance. With his encouragement, she went to New York to become a writer. Charlotte Osgood Mason, whom Hurston sarcastically called "Godmother," was a good friend and patron of Locke's and provided financial assistance to Hurston. However, Mason's patronage had a price, and Hurston was often frustrated by the constraints put on her by Mason. Hurston was given little money by Mason. Moreover, Hurston, known for her frequently outrageous behavior, was often chastised and threatened by the possibility of being dismissed by Mason.

In addition to writing novels, Hurston was a folklorist. She traveled the rural South collecting folklore from African Americans. Hurston also collaborated with Langston Hughes. After the decline of the Harlem Renaissance, Hurston was accused of an illicit affair with a young boy. Even though she was acquitted in court, the scandal ruined her career, and Hurston died penniless in a Florida nursing home.

Nella Larsen

Nella Larsen was born in 1891 in Chicago. Her mother was Danish and her father was West Indian. When Larsen arrived in New York, she worked as a nurse and as a librarian. She wrote *Passing* and *Quicksand*, two popular Renaissance novels that dealt with the theme of the tragic mulatto. She then left the Harlem scene to resume her career in nursing. Much of her later life remained a mystery until recently.

Florence Mills

Florence Mills made her stage debut at the age of four and worked in show business her entire life. She was a star in *Shuffle Along*, causing a sensation every night when she sang. She appeared in many revues and also toured Europe. She was truly an international star. Mills was multitalented and loved by her many fans. Unfortunately, she died tragically at the height of her career when she was only 26 years old.

Augusta Savage

Augusta Savage was born in Florida. She began playing with the red Florida clay as a child, and as she grew older, her talent as a sculptor became evident. With the help of a benefactor, she went to New York to study and, after overcoming many obstacles, began to gain recognition. She sculpted busts of W. E. B. Du Bois, Marcus Garvey, and W. C. Handy.

Bessie Smith

Bessie Smith was born in Chattanooga, Tennessee, in 1894. She began touring with traveling shows and soon earned a reputation for her singing. By the 1920s, she was the top blues singer in the country. Billed as "The Empress of the Blues," Smith is still considered by many to be the best blues singer ever. Even in the 1920s, her records were big sellers. This was quite an accomplishment at a time when Blacks were ignored by the recording industry. She was always a popular attraction in Harlem during the Renaissance. She died at age 42 as a result of a car accident.

Ethel Waters

Ethel Waters was born in Chester, Pennsylvania. Life was hard for a child living in the red-light district. She left home as soon as she could and began singing in Baltimore; however, she quickly moved to New York. She was known as "Sweet Mama Stringbean" and sang seductive songs when she appeared at the Cotton Club, on

Broadway, and at several other Harlem nightclubs. Later in her career, she worked as an actress in movies and television. Waters was nominated for an Academy Award in 1950.

**Fig. 5.2.
Ethel Waters (Schomburg Center, NYPL).**

Elida Webb

Elida Webb was both a dancer and a choreographer. She made a name for herself as a dancer in *Shuffle Along*, the Broadway show that many felt was one of the catalysts of the Harlem Renaissance. She was then hired as choreographer for *Runnin' Wild*, the show that introduced the world to the Charleston. For many years she worked at the Cotton Club as choreographer, the first African American to work there in that capacity. Her later life was tinged with sadness. Elida Webb was an original and made many contributions to the field of dance.

Use the sources below to learn more about the lives and achievements made by the women of the Harlem Renaissance.

Bibliography

Albertson, Chris. **Bessie**. New York: Stein and Day, 1985. 253p. $8.95. ISBN 0-8128-1700-1.

Albertson has been involved with Bessie Smith's life and career for many years, having won Grammies for working on the Columbia Records reissues of her work. In fact, he is probably more responsible than any other writer for keeping her memory alive. Smith's life and career are fascinating; she was raucous, outspoken, and fun-loving. She was also one of the best blues singers ever and influenced many modern singers. Albertson does a fine job of capturing her personality in this book. He also includes personal recollections of many who knew and worked with her. Thoroughly researched and well written, this book traces Smith's rise to fame, her personal ups and downs, and her tragic death in 1937. Several black-and-white photographs complete the volume. This book is written for adults, but is equally suitable for students in grades 7 through 12.

Albertson, Chris, comp. **Bessie Smith: Empress of the Blues**. New York: Macmillan, 1975. 143p. ISBN 0-028-70020-1.

Albertson, a widely known and respected jazz historian, wrote this book for younger readers. Although it is not available at this time, it is included here for several reasons. It is a beautifully designed book, the large black-and-white photographs of Smith are striking, and it is possible that copies of the book may be available in a public or school library. Certainly, it is well worth looking for. The book begins with a biography of Bessie Smith's life. In addition to the photographs, there are reprints of ads from Columbia Records and the Lafayette Theatre, stills from the film *St. Louis Blues*, and several photographs taken by Carl Van Vechten. There are also several pages of music and lyrics from Smith's songs and a reprint of an original manuscript of the song "Pickpocket Blues." This is an excellent, well-written source for those who like the blues or who want to learn more about Bessie Smith. Appropriate for grades 4 through 9.

Anderson, Marian. **My Lord, What a Morning**. Introduction by Nellie McKay. Madison, WI: The University of Wisconsin Press, 1992. Reprint. 348p. $37.50. ISBN 0-299-13390-7.

Anderson's autobiography was originally published in 1956. She writes of her childhood in Philadelphia, her studies, and her debut at Town Hall in New York during the Harlem Renaissance. Although the concert was a disaster, Anderson continued to work hard and finally achieved success. Anderson's book details many racial incidents throughout her life. One incident involved her denial of entrance to a music school. Anderson merely recounts the incidents; her feelings are not revealed. Also, Anderson makes no mention of the political or social climate of the times in which she lived and worked. Despite the lack of such revelations, Anderson's book makes clear that she made many contributions to the concert world and undoubtedly paved the way for many other African Americans. McKay's introduction offers insights into what may seem like omissions on Anderson's part. McKay cites the qualities of dignity and humility that guided not only Anderson's writing, but her entire life. McKay further suggests that it is Anderson's quality of dignity that made her victorious over those who sought to stop her. Recommended for grades 7 through 12 and above.

Bogle, Donald. **Brown Sugar: Eighty Years of America's Black Female Stars**. New York: Da Capo, 1990. 208p. $15.95. ISBN 0-306-80380-1.

Bogle explores the history of African American women in show business, with his premise being that each of his subjects is a diva with style. This premise is made clear in part as Bogle profiles blues singer Ma Rainey, popular in the early 1900s prior to the Harlem Renaissance, as the forerunner of all divas in later decades. Bogle's section devoted to the 1920s focuses on blues singers in general and Bessie Smith in particular. He provides biographical sketches of Florence Mills, Josephine Baker, Ethel Waters, and Nina Mae McKinney, all performers during the Harlem Renaissance. There is also an interesting section on chorus girls. Included are many black-and-white photographs and illustrations. Bogle's specialty is African Americans in film, and as with his other works, this one is well researched and clearly written. Information here, especially in the section on chorus girls, will not be found in other sources. Recommended for grades 7 through 12 and above.

Davis, Thadious M. **Nella Larsen, Novelist of the Harlem Renaissance: A Woman's Life Unveiled**. Baton Rouge, LA: Louisiana State University Press, 1994. 494p. $34.95. ISBN 0-8071-1866-4.

Davis became interested in Nella Larsen because she was such a mystery. He began tracing her life, only to discover that Larsen, herself, was largely responsible for the mystery. By 1935, she had disappeared from the literary scene. Davis's thorough research covers her childhood, including name changes and her mother's denial of her birth. Larsen eventually moved to New York City, where she found work as a nurse and also began to write. For a time she also worked at the 135th Street branch of the New York Public Library. Davis uncovers details of Larsen's life and career and offers an explanation for her elusive lifestyle. Appendixes include a bibliography of reviews and a chronological listing of her work. The index is excellent. Ideal for grades 10 through 12 and above.

Harrison, Daphne Duval. **Black Pearls: Blues Queens of the 1920s**. New Brunswick, NJ: Rutgers University Press, 1988. 225p. $13.95. ISBN 0-8135-1280-8.

More than a selection of profiles of blues singers, Harrison's work is a social history of the era as well. She discusses the effects of the Great Migration on African American women's lives and on the blues. Harrison also details the impact of the birth of the recording industry and the Theatre Owner's Booking Association on these women and their music. The author delves into the lives of female blues singers. Edith Wilson, Alberta Hunter, Victoria Spivey, and Sippie Wallace are all discussed at length. Styles and lyrics are also examined. Of particular interest are the chapters on Hunter and Wilson, in which Harrison details their involvement in and contributions to the Harlem Renaissance. In an appendix, "Other Blues Singers," Harrison provides one- to two-page profiles of lesser-known blues singers of the era. Selected titles, glossary, and bibliography are also included, as are black-and-white photographs.

Although only a small section of this work may seem relevant to the Harlem Renaissance, it is an important source for its discussion of the role of African American women in society or at least in one aspect of it during the era. Recommended for grades 7 through 12 and above.

Hemenway, Robert E. **Zora Neale Hurston: A Literary Biography**. Urbana, IL: University of Illinois Press, 1978. 371p. $12.50. ISBN 0-252-00807-3.

Hemenway's excellent biography covers Hurston's life, captures her vivacious spirit, and provides an interpretation of her works. Chapter 2, "Harlem City," deals with Hurston's involvement in the Harlem Renaissance. Chapter 5, "Godmother and Big Sweet," details Hurston's relationship with her patron, Charlotte Osgood Mason. These details of Hurston's life can be found elsewhere, but Hemenway combines lucid, engaging narrative with superb literary criticism. This thoroughly researched book includes black-and-white photographs and wonderful details of Hurston's adventures collecting folklore. Recommended for grades 10 through 12 and above.

Hine, Darlene Clark, Elsa Barkley Brown, and Rosalyn Terborg-Penn, eds. **Black Women in America: An Historical Encyclopedia**. Brooklyn, NY: Carlson, 1993. 1,600p. $195.00. ISBN 0-926019-61-9.

This two-volume set contains biographical sketches of 641 women and approximately 160 general topics, one of which is the Harlem Renaissance. "See also" references direct readers to individual sketches. The section on the Harlem Renaissance provides useful information on the female role in the movement and includes women who made contributions from all walks of life—women who may not be found in other works. Sketches provide personal and career information. Several black-and-white photographs enhance this set. Arranged alphabetically, subject matter is easily accessible. The set can be used by adults and students in grades 7 through 12 interested in Black history or women's studies.

Hull, Gloria T. **Color, Sex, and Poetry: Three Women Writers of the Harlem Renaissance**. Bloomington, IN: Indiana State University Press, 1987. 242p. $35.00. ISBN 0-253-34974-5.

Hull's introduction discusses the Harlem Renaissance and women's place in it. She also discusses the social politics of Harlem Renaissance writers, patronage, and the personal and professional lives of her three subjects: Alice Dunbar Nelson, Angelina Weld Grimké, and Georgia Douglas Johnson. Hull provides thorough analyses of her three poets. She finds some similarities among them; all were of racially mixed blood, all wrote lyric poetry, and all wrote forms of prose. Since these writers do not receive the same attention as some of their contemporaries, this is a welcome volume. Hull's writing is clear and lively, and her analyses are well done. This book is written for adults, but is also appropriate for students in grades 10 through 12.

Jordan, Caspar Leroy, comp. **A Bibliographical Guide to African-American Women Writers**. Vol. 31 of Bibliographies of Indexes and Indexes in Afro-American Studies. Westport, CT: Greenwood, 1993. 416p. $65.00. ISBN 0-313-27633-1.

Several entries in this bibliography cover women who were active in the Harlem Renaissance. This comprehensive volume also covers many of the more obscure writers who may not be found in other volumes. Arranged alphabetically by author, each entry covers primary and secondary works. The bibliographies are generally well done. This is an excellent starting point for research. It is a worthwhile source for grades 10 through 12 and above.

Lyons, Mary E. **Sorrow's Kitchen: The Life and Folklore of Zora Neale Hurston**. New York: Charles Scribner's Sons, 1990. 160p. $14.95. ISBN 0-684-19198-9.

Lyons's book is clearly written and well researched. It includes black-and-white photographs and excerpts of Hurston's folklore. The book is rich in detail of Hurston's personal and professional life. The chapters on the Harlem Renaissance offer interesting accounts of Hurston's relationship with her patron, her introduction to the world of the Harlem Renaissance at an awards dinner, and her falling-out with Langston Hughes. Written for grades 5 through 9.

Patterson, Charles. **Marian Anderson**. Impact Biography Series. New York: Franklin Watts, 1988. 160p. $15.47. ISBN 0-531-10568-7.

This is a well-written biography of Marian Anderson's life. In addition to describing her childhood, her training, and her career, the book details her efforts to overcome prejudice. Photographs are included in the book, as well as a chronology of important events in Anderson's life. Patterson's writing is straightforward and engaging and will appeal to students in grades 7 through 10.

Roses, Lorraine Elena, and Ruth Elizabeth Randolph. **Harlem Renaissance and Beyond: Literary Biographies of 100 Black Women Writers 1900–1945**. Boston: G. K. Hall, 1990. 536p. $45.00. ISBN 0-8161-8926-9.

This source profiles women's lives and works. It contains approximately 100 biographical essays, as well as lists of primary and secondary titles. An extensive bibliography concludes the book. What makes this title stand out is its biographical essays. They are insightful, in-depth portraits that link the author's work to the time period, thus adding a context of social history to the lives and works of each subject. There are many references to the women of the Harlem Renaissance. Designed for researchers in women's studies or Black studies, the book can also be used by young adults.

Schroeder, Alan. **Josephine Baker**. Black Americans of Achievement Series. New York: Chelsea House, 1991. 128p. $17.95. ISBN 0-7910-1116-X.

Written in clear, straightforward language, this biography traces Josephine Baker's life and career. From approximately 1922 to 1925, Baker appeared in many shows in New York, including *Shuffle Along*. She was an immediate hit before going to Paris in 1925. This book provides many details and photographs of the pre-Paris period of her career. Her life is fascinating, as the many black-and-white photographs in this book make clear. The photographs also show the many facets of Baker's talent. This book is part of an excellent series written for readers in grades 7 through 10.

Sylvander, Carolyn Wedin. **Jessie Redmon Fauset, Black American Writer**. Troy, NY: Whitston Publishing, 1981. 276p. ISBN 0-87875-196-3.

Sylvander's work offers more than biographical information on Fauset. In addition to discussing Fauset's skill as an editor at *The Crisis*, official publication of National Association for the Advancement of Colored People (NAACP), Sylvander critiques Fauset's novels, which she believes are often wrongly maligned. The premise of Sylvander's work is that details of Fauset's life would reveal her character, her struggles against racism and sexism, and the connection between her life and her work. Sylvander parallels strengths and weaknesses of Fauset's character with those of her writing. Appropriate for students in grades 10 through 12 and above.

Tedards, Ann. **Marian Anderson**. American Women of Achievement Series. New York: Chelsea House, 1988. 112p. $17.95. ISBN 1-55546-638-9.

Tedards, herself a professional singer, puts her musical background to good use in this well-researched and clearly written book. Chapters 1 and 2 are significant to those interested in the Harlem Renaissance. They trace Anderson's childhood in Philadelphia, her success performing in Harlem, and her experiences with racism. The support she received from Roland Hayes, an African American concert singer who gained respect after successfully touring Europe, then achieved fame in the United States, is detailed as well. The book features an excellent selection of black-and-white photographs, a chronology of significant events in Anderson's career, and a bibliography. Written for grades 7 through 12.

Wall, Cheryl A. **Women of the Harlem Renaissance**. Women of Letters Series. Bloomington, IN: Indiana State University Press, 1995. 246p. $32.35. ISBN 0-253-32908-6.

Wall has chosen Jessie Fauset, Nella Larsen, and Zora Neale Hurston as the subjects of her book. She opens with a discussion of race and gender, contrasting Alain Locke's perspective of the Harlem Renaissance and the "New Negro"—a term used to identify educated, urban Blacks—with an essay by Marita Bonner, whose work was published by her daughter after her death. Bonner's work offers a female perspective of the Renaissance, which sets the tone for Wall's profiles of her three subjects. Wall's work is straightforward and objective; her profile of Jessie Fauset, managing editor of *The Crisis*, cites flaws and weaknesses in Fauset's writing. Her discussion of Larsen includes the issue of color and the accusation of plagiarism that affected Larsen's career. She also discusses Larsen's use of the theme of the "tragic mulatto" in her work. Wall likens Hurston to a blues singer, one who is often searching. Unlike Larson and Fauset, Hurston recorded language of real people. Hurston's association with her patron, Charlotte Mason, affected not only her work but her daily life. Wall provides details of Hurston's agreement with Mason. Wall also analyzes each writer's major works. Coverage is thorough, and the book's discussion of gender makes it an important resource. Written for adults, but appropriate for students in grades 10 through 12.

Waters, Ethel, with Charles Samuels. **His Eye Is on the Sparrow**. Westport, CT: Greenwood, 1978. Reprint. 304p. $13.95. ISBN 0-306-80477-8.

Ethel Waters was a popular performer on Broadway, at the Cotton Club, and later, in films and on television. The song "Stormy Weather" was written for her by George Gershwin. She writes in detail about these events in her life. She also writes of her childhood of poverty and violence and tells how she saw her way out of it by winning singing contests, working in vaudeville, and finally achieving success in New York during the Harlem Renaissance. Included in this book are remembrances of her colleagues. Several black-and-white photographs complement the text. Written for adults, this book is also appropriate for students in grades 10 through 12.

Werner, Craig. **Black American Women Novelists: An Annotated Bibliography**. Magill Bibliographies Series. Metuchen, NJ: Scarecrow Press, 1989. 286p. $40.00. ISBN 0-8108-2787-5.

The introduction to this work contains approximately 250 citations to books, articles, and sources. The main section contains annotated citations of the works of 33 novelists, some of whom were Harlem Renaissance writers. In addition, Werner lists works of biography and general commentary about each author. The book is worth reading for Werner's introduction alone, which is insightful and thorough. Designed for adult researchers, but students in grades 10 through 12 will find it easy to use.

Witcover, Paul. **Zora Neale Hurston**. Black Americans of Achievement Series. New York: Chelsea House, 1991. 112p. $17.95. ISBN 0-7910-1129-1.

Clearly written, Witcover's book profiles Zora Neale Hurston's life and times. A large number of black-and-white photographs chronicle Hurston's private and professional life. Photos of Hurston and her contemporaries make this an excellent biography. A bibliography of the author's works and a chronology of important events in her life round out the book. This is an excellent example of a biography written for students in grades 7 through 10.

Part III

Literature and Writing

LITERATURE

More has been written about the literature of the Harlem Renaissance than about any other aspect of it. More and more works of these writers are being rediscovered. Zora Neale Hurston's work is enjoying new popularity. Wallace Thurman's work is available in paperback, and Nella Larsen has also received recognition via a recent biography. Dorothy West published a novel in 1995. Websites can be found for Langston Hughes, Jean Toomer, and Zora Neale Hurston.

During their life times, the Renaissance writers received recognition largely through the efforts of Carl Van Vechten, who was responsible for publishing many of their works. They also supported each other and received support from patrons and other wealthy devotees.

Salons

Salons were a means of helping Harlem Renaissance writers and artists gain recognition and of introducing them to publishers or to wealthy patrons who would lend financial aid. Those who established salons were usually wealthy and influential; they had the power to attract others like themselves. Guests often vied for invitations. Salons were also established by the writers, themselves; however, the nature of these salons was to provide support, feedback, and, when necessary, a haven.

A'Lelia Walker, daughter of beauty entrepreneur Madame C. J. Walker, organized a literary salon at her home. Her intention was to offer a place for all young Black artists and writers to discuss and exhibit their work. Named after Countee Cullen's column in *Opportunity*, a literary publication, Walker's salon was known as the Dark Tower. Works by Countee Cullen and Langston Hughes decorated the walls.

Other salons were organized by Carl Van Vechten and Georgia Douglas Johnson. Wallace Thurman held court at "Niggerati Manor," a salon for his friends, many of whom were considered avant-garde. Although these salons were an important part of the social history of the Renaissance, it is also important to look at the works of those who gathered there.

Countee Cullen

Countee Cullen, a poet, was born in New York City in 1903. He was orphaned in his teens and adopted by Rev. Frederick Cullen. Cullen was well educated; he was a Phi Beta Kappa graduate of New York University and, later, a graduate of Harvard University. He won several awards for his writing, including an *Opportunity* poetry contest, a Harmon Foundation award, and a Guggenheim Fellowship.

Cullen's marriage to Yolande Du Bois, daughter of W. E. B. Du Bois, was well publicized, but the marriage ended in divorce after only a year. After the decline of the Harlem Renaissance, Cullen taught school in Harlem. His writing often dealt with themes related to Africa. He published several books of poetry, including *Color, The Black Christ and Other Poems*, and *The Ballad of the Brown Girl*. He died in 1946.

Jessie Fauset

Jessie Fauset, herself a writer, edited *The Crisis*, the official publication of the National Association for the Advancement of Colored People (NAACP). In this capacity, she worked closely with W. E. B. Du Bois. Although she is more widely known as a novelist, she excelled as an editor. She was largely responsible for discovering the talents of many Harlem Renaissance writers, including Langston Hughes, Countee Cullen, and Jean Toomer. Fauset was also responsible for *The Brownie's Book*, a magazine for children that was published during the Harlem Renaissance. Her novels include *There Is Confusion*, *Plum Bun*, and *The Chinaberry Tree*.

Langston Hughes

Langston Hughes was born in Joplin, Missouri, in 1902. He traveled to Mexico and Europe, working his way on freighters, before arriving in New York City in the early 1920s. Hughes was a prolific writer and a skilled poet, novelist, playwright, and songwriter. He wrote for children as well as for adults. He is credited as being one of the first writers of the Harlem Renaissance. His poetry dealt with themes of blues and, later, with social protest. He used folklore and humor often in his work. His works include *Weary Blues*, *Not Without Laughter*, *The Ways of White Folks*, and a two-volume autobiography, *The Big Sea* and *I Wonder as I Wander*. Hughes died in 1967.

Zora Neale Hurston

Zora Neale Hurston was born in Florida in 1903. She studied at Howard University, and with Alain Locke's encouragement, she went to New York to become a writer. Charlotte Osgood Mason, whom Hurston called "Godmother," provided financial assistance to Hurston. However, Mason's patronage had a price, and Hurston was often frustrated by the constraints put on her by Mason.

In addition to writing novels, Hurston was a folklorist. She traveled the rural South collecting folklore from African Americans. Hurston also collaborated with Langston Hughes. After the decline of the Harlem Renaissance, a scandal ruined her career, and Hurston died penniless in a Florida nursing home.

Nella Larsen

Nella Larsen was born in 1891 in Chicago. Her mother was Danish and her father was West Indian. When Larsen arrived in New York she worked as a nurse and as a librarian. She wrote *Passing* and *Quicksand*, two popular Renaissance novels that dealt with the theme of the tragic mulatto. She then left the Harlem scene to resume her career in nursing. Much of her later life remained a mystery until recently.

Claude McKay

Claude McKay was born in Jamaica in 1890. He published two volumes of poetry before immigrating to the United States. He studied briefly at Tuskegee Institute and at Kansas State University before moving to New York City to become a writer. In 1922, he published *Harlem Shadows*, a book of poetry that has been credited by some as the work that brought about the Harlem Renaissance. McKay was considered a radical and often at odds with his contemporaries. In addition to his poetry, McKay published novels, among them, *Home to Harlem* and *Banjo*.

Wallace Thurman

Thurman was born in 1902 in Salt Lake City, Utah, and arrived in Harlem in the mid-1920s. His play *Harlem: A Melodrama of Negro Life in Harlem* was a success on Broadway. Thurman also wrote three novels. One of them, *The Blacker the Berry*, was reissued in paperback in 1970 and is still available. Thurman was only 34 years old when he died from tuberculosis. He was considered bohemian by many of his contemporaries and lived a destructive lifestyle.

The following are excellent references to the works of Harlem Renaissance writers.

Biblioqraphy

Barksdale, Richard, and Kenneth Kinnamon. **Black Writers of America**. New York: Macmillan, 1972. 980p. $74.00. ISBN 0-02-306080-8.

Part 5 of this book, beginning on page 468, covers writers of the Harlem Renaissance. The introduction provides an excellent overview of the events that led to the Harlem Renaissance and covers social, economic, and political aspects of the era as well. Writers profiled are discussed in the introduction in terms of their contributions to the movement. This is an excellent source for those who wish to learn about the factors that led to the Harlem Renaissance. It is also a good starting point for research. Written for adults, it is an easy-to-use reference for students in grades 7 through 12 as well.

Berry, Faith. **Langston Hughes: Before and Beyond Harlem**. Westport, CT: Lawrence Hill and Company, 1983. 376p. $15.95. ISBN 0-88208-156-X.

Berry's work is based on primary and secondary sources. She managed to interview Arna Bontemps, Roland Hayes, Clarence Muse, Paul Robeson, and William Grant Still, all contemporaries of Langston Hughes.

Much of Berry's book focuses on Hughes's personal and professional life before the 1940s. Details of Countee Cullen's marriage to Yolande Du Bois, patron Charlotte Osgood Mason's influence on Hughes and Alain Locke, and Hughes's conflict with Zora Neale Hurston are all here. Written as a narrative, Berry's work provides biographical information and details of Hughes's personal life and professional development as a writer. Appropriate for adults and students in grades 7 through 12.

Bloom, Harold, ed. **Black American Poets and Dramatists of the Harlem Renaissance**. Writers of English: Lives and Works Series. New York: Chelsea House, 1995. 160p. $29.95. ISBN 0-7910-2207-2.

————. **Black American Prose Writers of the Harlem Renaissance**. Writers of English: Lives and Works Series. New York: Chelsea House, 1994. 174p. $29.95. ISBN 0-7910-2203-X.

These two works are companion pieces; they are arranged exactly alike. Bloom not only examines writers, such as Langston Hughes, Countee Cullen, Claude McKay, and Jean Toomer, he also includes lesser-known writers, such as Sterling A. Brown, Randolph Edmonds, Abram Hill, and Frank Wilson. Bloom provides biographical sketches for each writer, highlighting significant events in his or her life. Each writer's major works are listed as well. Critical extracts are arranged chronologically and range widely in their focus and point of view. Critiques range from those of the authors' contemporaries to those of modern writers. Bloom's books are excellent resources; they are informative, appealing, and hard to put down. Recommended for adults and students in grades 7 through 12.

Bontemps, Arna, ed. **The Harlem Renaissance Remembered**. New York: Dodd, Mead, 1972. 310p. $9.95. ISBN 0-396-08432-X.

Bontemps, a poet active during the Harlem Renaissance, compiled this study of various aspects of the movement. In addition to Bontemps's work, there are essays by several scholars. The work opens with his own recounting of the era, including his arrival in Harlem, his introduction to Countee Cullen, and a party where Langston Hughes was guest of honor. Also included are profiles of Cullen, Thurman, and Toomer. There is an excellent profile of Charles S. Johnson as well, which includes information not found elsewhere. Patricia Turner's profile of Langston Hughes is rich in detail. Mae Gwendolyn Henderson's study of Wallace Thurman is an excellent source of information as well. Notes and bibliographies appear with each essay. That Bontemps, himself, was active during the Harlem Renaissance makes this an excellent choice for a firsthand historical perspective of the era. Recommended for adults and students in grades 10 through 12.

Cooper, Wayne F. **Claude McKay: Rebel Sojourner in the Harlem Renaissance**. Baton Rouge, LA: Louisiana State University Press, 1987. 443p. $34.95. ISBN 0-8071-1310-7.

Claude McKay, born in Jamaica, is considered in writing circles to be an innovator. Cooper's introduction discusses McKay's contribution to and place in African American literature. Cooper agrees with many others who believe that McKay's poetry of protest marked the beginning of the Harlem Renaissance. McKay's personal and professional life is covered, beginning with his birth in Jamaica, his later years in the United States, England, and Russia, and finally his conversion to Catholicism. Cooper's biography is fascinating in that he achieves his goal of revealing McKay's personality. Extensive research notes, an essay on sources, and an index complete the volume. This book is written for adults, but is suitable for students in grades 10 through 12 as well.

Davis, Arthur P. **From the Dark Tower: African American Writers from 1900–1960**. Washington, DC: Howard University Press, 1981. 306p. $19.50. ISBN 088258-004-3.

This volume examines major African American writers from the period prior to the Harlem Renaissance through 1960. Part 1 covers the period 1900–40. The introduction gives a social and a literary background. It is arranged in chronological order with each author's works listed in order of importance. Also featured is a selective bibliography of primary and secondary works for each author discussed, along with photographs of each author, many of which were taken by Carl Van Vechten. Included are Wallace Thurman, Countee Cullen, Claude McKay, Rudolph Fisher, James Weldon Johnson, Jessie Fauset, Nella Larsen, and George Schuyler. Davis, a professor at Howard University, has created a series of perceptive sketches. The book is designed for students in grades 10 through 12 and above, but the straightforward writing and arrangement make it suitable for grades 7 through 10.

Davis, Thadious M. **Nella Larsen, Novelist of the Harlem Renaissance: A Woman's Life Unveiled**. Baton Rouge, LA: Louisiana State University Press, 1994. 494p. $34.95. ISBN 0-8071-1866-4.

Davis became interested in Nella Larsen because she was such a mystery. He began tracing her life, only to discover that Larsen, herself, was largely responsible for the mystery. By 1935, she had disappeared from the literary scene. Davis's thorough research covers her childhood, including name changes and her mother's denial of her birth. Trained as a nurse, Larsen moved to New York City and also began to write. For a time she worked at the 135th Street branch of the New York Public Library. Davis's detailed research of Larsen's life and career concludes with an explanation of her elusive lifestyle. Appendixes include a bibliography of reviews of her work and a chronological listing of her works. The index is excellent. Ideal for adults and students in grades 10 through 12.

Estell, Kenneth, ed. "Literature." In vol. 4 of **Reference Library of Black America**. Detroit, MI: Gale Research, 1993. 1600p. $179.00. ISBN 0-685-49222-2.

Each section of Estell's work opens with an essay that focuses on the historical perspective of the topic. Each chapter ends with biographical profiles. Several illustrations are included. An extensive bibliography lists works by topic. Estell's volume provides an overview of the literature of the era, with a slant on the social history of the Renaissance. Profiles are brief, but informative and clearly written. Recommended for students in grades 7 through 12.

Harris, Trudier, and Thadious M. Davis, eds. **Afro-American Writers: The Harlem Renaissance to 1940**. Dictionary of Literary Biography Series. Detroit, MI: Gale Research, 1987. 386p. $128.00. ISBN 0-8103-1729-X.

Biographical data are provided on Harlem Renaissance writers from James Weldon Johnson to Wallace Thurman. Each essay begins with a list of works by the profiled author, followed by a discussion of the writer's life and works; the essay concludes with selected references to critical works. Also included are excellent photographs of each writer. The Dictionary of Literary Biography Series is respected, and this volume lives up to its name. Recommended for students in grades 7 through 12 and above.

Hedgepeth, Chester. **Twentieth-Century African-American Writers and Artists**. Chicago: American Library Association, 1991. 336p. $50.00. ISBN 0-8389-0534-X.

Artists, writers, and musicians are profiled in this work. Each sketch is one to one-and-a-half pages long. Sketches include biographies, selected lists of primary and secondary works, and critiques. Nearly 250 subjects are listed. Sketches are informative, and the book is fairly comprehensive. Profiles include those of Harlem Renaissance writers Langston Hughes, Countee Cullen, and Claude McKay. This is a good starting point for research. Recommended for students in grades 7 through 12 and above.

Hemenway, Robert E. **Zora Neale Hurston: A Literary Biography**. Urbana, IL: University of Illinois Press, 1978. 371p. $12.50. ISBN 0-252-00807-3.

Hemenway's excellent biography covers Zora Neale Hurston's life, captures her vivacious spirit, and provides an interpretation of her works. Chapter 2, "Harlem City," deals with Hurston's involvement in the Harlem Renaissance. Chapter 5, "Godmother and Big Sweet," details Hurston's relationship with her patron, Charlotte Osgood Mason. These details of Hurston's life can be found elsewhere, but Hemenway combines lucid, engaging narrative with superb literary criticism. This thoroughly researched work includes black-and-white photographs. There are also wonderful details of Hurston's adventures collecting folklore. Recommended for adults and students in grades 10 through 12.

Hughes, Langston. **The Big Sea: An Autobiography**. New York: Hill and Wang, 1993. 335p. $14.00. ISBN 0-809-01549-8.

Hughes wrote his autobiography in two volumes. This first volume covers the Harlem Renaissance. Part 3, "Black Renaissance," begins with a description of social life in Harlem, dancing at the Savoy, and Saturday night rent parties. The popularity of rent parties lasted long after the Harlem Renaissance. Anyone could give a rent party, as long as there was music, good food, and drink. Guests paid an admission fee, which was applied to the host's monthly rent. Hughes goes on to describe Countee Cullen's marriage to Yolande Du Bois and Florence Mills's funeral. Hughes presents a true first-hand account of the era. He writes at length about his contemporaries, Wallace Thurman, Zora Neale Hurston, and Arna Bontemps, among others. Also included are some of Hughes's poems. His writing style and use of language are unsurpassed. Hughes's work is excellent as social history and as literature. Recommended for adults and for students in grades 7 through 12.

Hull, Gloria T. **Color, Sex, and Poetry: Three Women Writers of the Harlem Renaissance**. Bloomington, IN: Indiana State University Press, 1987. 242p. $35.00. ISBN 0-253-34974-5.

Hull's introduction discusses the Harlem Renaissance and women's place in it. She also discusses the social politics of Harlem Renaissance writers, patronage, and the personal and professional lives of her three subjects: Alice Dunbar Nelson, Angelina Weld Grimké, and Georgia Douglas Johnson. Hull provides thorough analyses of her three poets. She finds some similarities among them; all were of racially mixed blood, all wrote lyric poetry, and all wrote forms of prose. Since these writers do not receive the same attention as some of their contemporaries, this is a welcome volume. Hull's writing is clear and lively, and her analyses are well done. Written for adults but also appropriate for students in grades 10 through 12.

Inge, M. Thomas. **The Beginnings Through the Harlem Renaissance and Langston Hughes**. Vol. 1 of Black American Writers: Bibliographical Essays. New York: St. Martin's Press, 1978. 216p. ISBN 0-3120-8260-6.

This volume provides an overview of the lives and careers of the authors profiled. Each chapter begins with an introduction, then presents bibliographical essays on each subject. The book is currently out of print, but it is included here for two important reasons: It lists biographical and critical writings related to each writer, and it includes bibliographies of manuscripts and letters. It provides a fairly thorough coverage of Harlem Renaissance writers. The book is written for adults, but students in grades 10 through 12 will find it easily accessible.

Jordan, Caspar Leroy, comp. **A Bibliographical Guide to African-American Women Writers**. Vol. 31 of Bibliographies of Indexes and Indexes in Afro-American Studies. Westport, CT: Greenwood, 1993. 416p. $65.00. ISBN 0-313-27633-1.

Several entries in this bibliography cover women who were active in the Harlem Renaissance. This comprehensive volume also covers many of the more obscure writers who may not be found in other volumes. Arranged alphabetically by author, each entry lists primary and secondary works. The bibliographies are generally well done. This is an excellent starting point for research for adults and students in grades 10 through 12.

Kerman, Cynthia Earl. **The Lives of Jean Toomer: A Hunger for Wholeness**. Baton Rouge, LA: Louisiana State University Press, 1987. 411p. $16.95. ISBN 0-8071-1354-9.

Toomer's novel *Cane* brought him prominence during the Harlem Renaissance; it was one of the first novels published during the era. However, Toomer did not remain an active participant in the Renaissance. Little is known about his life; he seems both mysterious and complex. Kerman attempts to solve the mystery of Toomer's life through Toomer's own journals, correspondence, and other writings, as well as through interviews with those who knew him. Toomer left Harlem after the publication of *Cane* to devote his life to the teachings of his spiritual leader, Georges Gurdjieff. He later became a Quaker. Yet *Cane* had a profound effect on the Harlem Renaissance and was often referred to as a masterpiece by Toomer's contemporaries. Although little of this work focuses on the Harlem Renaissance, Toomer was an important writer of the era. Kerman's biography is thoroughly researched and contains details of Toomer's life not found elsewhere. Recommended for adults and students in grades 10 through 12.

Lyons, Mary E. **Sorrow's Kitchen: The Life and Folklore of Zora Neale Hurston**. New York: Charles Scribner's Sons, 1990. 160p. $14.95. ISBN 0-684-19198-9.

Lyons's book is clearly written and well researched. It includes black-and-white photographs and excerpts of Hurston's folklore. The book is rich in detail of Hurston's personal and professional life. The chapters on the Harlem Renaissance offer interesting accounts of Hurston's relationship with her patron, her introduction to the world of the Harlem Renaissance at an awards dinner, and her falling-out with Langston Hughes. Written for students in grades 4 through 9.

Magill, Frank N., ed. **Masterpieces of African-American Literature: Descriptions, Analyses, Characters, Plots, Themes, Critical Evaluations, and Significance of Major Works of Fiction, Non-Fiction, Drama and Poetry**. New York: Harper-Collins, 1992. 608p. $45.00. ISBN 0-06-270066-9.

Magill's works are well known to many students and teachers. This volume features critical summaries of works by nearly 100 African American writers. Each summary offers a brief analysis of theme, character, and setting. Essays are about 2,000 to 3,000 words each. This is a good source for those studying works of a particular author, for those comparing and contrasting authors' works, and for those interested in literary analysis. Recommended for students in grades 7 through 12.

Major, Clarence, ed. **The Garden Thrives: Twentieth Century African-American Poetry**. New York: HarperCollins, 1995. 470p. $17.00. ISBN 0-06-095-121-4.

Arranged chronologically by poet, Major's work is easily accessible. Several Harlem Renaissance authors' works are represented. Major's introduction offers an insightful discussion of poetry and, in particular, of Claude McKay and Alain Locke. The introduction, alone, makes this a worthy source for research. Works of both well-known and lesser-known poets of the period appear. Recommended for grades 7 through 12 and above.

McKay, Claude. **A Long Way from Home**. North Stratford, NH: Ayer, 1980. Reprint. 354p. $29.95. ISBN 0-405-01880-0.

Like Jean Toomer, Claude McKay was an important writer of the Harlem Renaissance who did not actually live in Harlem for most of the era. McKay, however, was outspoken, considered radical, and often at odds with W. E. B. Du Bois, Alain Locke, and other contemporaries. Much has been written about him. In his straightforward autobiography, McKay tells of his world travels and his interest in communism. Several sections are devoted to his interactions with Jessie Fauset, James Weldon Johnson, and Carl Van Vechten, among others. Appropriate for adults and students in grades 7 through 12.

Meltzer, Milton. "Harlem Poet." **Cobblestone** 12, no. 2 (February 1991): 10–14.

In this article Meltzer, an award-winning biographer, traces his friend Langston Hughes's arrival in Harlem in 1921. He also discusses Hughes's earlier years and his struggle to survive. The article includes photographs of Hughes, the staff of *Crisis* magazine, and the Lafayette Theatre. It is short but rich in social history. The focus is on Hughes, but the reader is also given a picture of Harlem, itself, during the Renaissance. The publication is designed for a younger audience; thus, the article is suitable for students in grades 4 through 9.

Metzger, Linda, ed. **Black Writers: A Selection of Sketches from Contemporary Authors Series**. Detroit, MI: Gale Research, 1993. 600p. $89.00. ISBN 0-8103-2772-4.

Entries provide personal and career data, bibliographies, and references to sources of further information. The "Sidelights" section provides details of each writer's critical reception. Photographs are included. Some nonliterary figures appear here, along with many writers of the Harlem Renaissance, such as Langston Hughes, Countee Cullen, Zora Neale Hurston, and Claude McKay. This book, a compilation of the popular, contemporary series is written for students in grades 7 through 12.

Mikolyzk, Thomas A., comp. **Langston Hughes: A Bio-Bibliography**. No. 2 of Bio-Bibliographies on Afro-Americans and Africans Series. Westport, CT: Greenwood, 1990. 288p. $45.00. ISBN 0-313-26895-9.

As the subtitle states, this is a bio-bibliography. The author's plan was to interweave notable events in Langston Hughes's personal life with the output of his literary works. The result is more emphasis on bibliography than on biography. The work also reflects Mikolyzk's personal opinions. After presenting a brief chronology, the author divides the text into works by Hughes and those about him. Author, title, and subject indexes and a coded bibliographic scheme make for easy access. This book is considered useful for students in grades 10 through 12 and above.

Mishkin, Tracey, ed. **Literary Influence and African American Writers**. Garland Library of the Humanities Series. New York: Garland, 1996. 389p. $73.00. ISBN 0-8153-1724-7.

Mishkin's curiosity about literary influence on and by Black writers prompted this collection of essays. Two essays relate to writers of the Harlem Renaissance. Brian Gallagher's "About Us, for Us, near Us: The Irish and Harlem Renaissances" cites many similarities in the two literary movements. He discusses lyricism in the poetry of William Butler Yeats and Langston Hughes. Mishkin's "How Black Sees Green and Red" provides examples of desire for social change in both literary movements and cites lack of recognition by the dominant culture as a significant factor in both Renaissances. Some readers may not agree with Gallagher and Mishkin, but their work is thought provoking and presents another point of view. Recommended for adults and students in grades 10 through 12.

Perry, Margaret. **The Harlem Renaissance**. Vol. 2 of Critical Studies on Black Life and Culture Series; Vol. 278 of Garland Reference Library of the Humanities. New York: Garland, 1982. 272p. ISBN 0-8240-9320-8.

This bibliography of works related to the Harlem Renaissance is thorough and well written. The annotations, alone, make this an excellent source of information. Perry's comprehensive introduction offers analyses of several authors' works. The book is arranged in four sections: "Bibliographic and Reference Material," "Literary Histories," "General Studies and Studies of Several Authors," and "Studies of Individual Authors." Each entry lists works by the author, reviews for each work, other writings, and writings about the author. Also included are miscellaneous articles, library and special collections, and dissertations. Recommended for students in grades 10 through 12 and above.

Roses, Lorraine Elena, and Ruth Elizabeth Randolph. **Harlem Renaissance and Beyond: Literary Biographies of 100 Black Women Writers 1900–1945**. Boston: G. K. Hall, 1990. 536p. $45.00. ISBN 0-8161-8926-9.

This source profiles women's lives and works. It contains approximately 100 biographical essays and lists of primary and secondary titles. An extensive bibliography concludes the book. What makes this title stand out is its biographical essays. They are insightful, in-depth portraits that link the author's work to the time period, thus adding a context of social history to the lives and works of each subject. There are many references to the women of the Harlem Renaissance. Designed for researchers in women's studies or Black studies, the book can also be used by students in grades 10 through 12.

Singh, Amritjit, William S. Shiver, and Stanley Brodwin. **The Harlem Renaissance: Revaluations**. Vol. 17 of Critical Studies on Black Life and Culture Series; Vol. 837 of Garland Reference Library of the Humanities Series. New York: Garland, 1989. 342p. ISBN 0-8340-5739-2.

This collection of papers presented at a 1985 conference devoted to the Harlem Renaissance presents a broad range of topics related to the era. Among selections presented are Primitivism, Bruce Kellner's profile of Carl Van Vechten, Arnold Rampersad's discussion of Langston Hughes as a modern poet, and Richard K. Barksdale's discussion of the theme of the tragic mulatto in Hughes's work. Also discussed is the controversy over jazz among intellectuals of the era. Many contributors to this volume are experts in their field. Recommended for students in grades 10 through 12 and above.

―――. **The Novels of the Harlem Renaissance**. University Park, PA: The Pennsylvania State University Press, 1976. 175p. ISBN 0-271-01208-0.

Singh has chosen to examine 21 novels written by African American authors and published between 1923–33. They include works by Arna Bontemps, Countee Cullen, W. E. B. Du Bois, Jessie Fauset, Langston Hughes, Nella Larsen, Claude McKay, and Wallace Thurman. Singh opens with a discussion of political, economic, cultural, and social aspects of the Harlem Renaissance. The novels, grouped according to themes, are then analyzed. Themes include race, class, and self-identity. Singh also includes a review of previous research and criticism, as well as a bibliography. Appropriate for students in grades 10 through 12 and above.

Storm, Doris, prod. **The Harlem Renaissance and Beyond**. Mt. Kisco, NY: Guidance Associates, 1969. $9.00. Videocassette, 35 min.

Part 1 of this filmstrip on videocassette focuses on writers of the Harlem Renaissance. Jean Toomer, Claude McKay, and Countee Cullen are mentioned briefly. Several excerpts of Langston Hughes's works are effectively read by Earle Hyman. The selections reflect the effect Harlem had on

Hughes and his fellow writers. Black-and-white photographs give a glimpse of life in Harlem during the 1920s. Modern color photographs are occasionally interspersed with the historically correct black-and-white photos, and little emphasis is placed on Hughes's contemporaries. Despite these flaws, the film accomplishes its goal of presenting Harlem, itself, as an important element of the Renaissance. Recommended for classroom presentations for grades 7 through 10.

Tillery, Tyrone. **Claude McKay: A Black Poet's Struggle for Identity**. Amherst, MA: University of Massachusetts Press, 1992. 235p. $30.00. ISBN 0-87023-762-4.

Tillery identifies conflicts surrounding the Harlem Renaissance and points to Claude McKay as the personification of these conflicts. McKay, proud of his humble background, denounced everything middle class. As a result, he often fought bitterly with W. E. B. Du Bois, particularly over editing and publication of his work in *The Crisis*. Alain Locke also attacked McKay as being disloyal to his race. Many details of McKay's interactions with other contemporaries are included as well. Tillery discusses McKay's works, his relationship with Marcus Garvey, and his conversion to Catholicism. This well-written work is recommended for adults and students in grades 10 through 12.

Tolson, Melvin B. ed. Afterword by Robert M. Farnsworth. **Gallery of Harlem Portraits**. Columbia, MO: University of Missouri Press, 1979. 288p. $32.00. ISBN 0-8262-0276-4.

Written during the Harlem Renaissance and completed in 1935, Tolson's work is modeled after Edgar Lee Masters's *Spoon River Anthology*. It presents lively portraits of life and people in Harlem. Each poem is a portrait of a Harlemite; many selections are thinly veiled portraits of actual people. "Peg-Leg Snelson" is clearly modeled after "Peg Leg" Bates, a popular dancer. "Abraham Dumas" is a fictionalized portrait of Alain Locke; "Percy Longfellow" is likewise a portrait of Countee Cullen. Poems represent points of view of individuals from all walks of life. They express sadness, anger, joy, complacency, bitterness, and humor. The book also includes a selection of black-and-white photographs. This is an excellent source of poetry for students in grades 7 through 12, as well as adult readers.

Tracey, Steven. **Langston Hughes and the Blues**. Urbana, IL: University of Illinois Press, 1988. 306p. $29.95. ISBN 0-252-01457-X.

Tracey, who holds a Ph.D. in English and is also a blues performer, opens his work with a discussion of folklore and its place in the literature of the Harlem Renaissance. He explains the origin of the blues and demonstrates Langston Hughes's use of blues structures, themes, and imagery in specific poems. Tracey's discussion of the Harlem Renaissance focuses on Zora Neale Hurston and Sterling Brown, both folklorists and contemporaries of Hughes. Tracey also analyzes W. E. B. Du Bois's, Alain Locke's, and James Weldon Johnson's conflicting views of folklore; the need for racial pride on one hand contradicted elitist views, concern over the proper African American image, and preference for White values on the other.

Tracey provides thorough background on the blues, detailed analyses of Hughes's poetry, and linkages between the two. Nonmusicians may become lost in some of the musical discussions; however, Tracey's work is unique and authoritative. Included are a bibliography and discography. Recommended for adults and students in grades 10 through 12.

Valade, Roger M., III, ed. with Denise Kasinec. **The Schomburg Center Guide to Black Literature: From the 18th Century to the Present**. Detroit, MI: Gale Research, 1996. 545p. $75.00. ISBN 0-7876-0289-2.

Designed as a ready reference, this work provides information on authors, works, characters, general themes, topics, and literary theories relating to Black literature. Coverage extends to literature topics, and even literary theories relating to the Harlem Renaissance. Entries include biographical essays, synopses of literary works, and essays on themes, terms, and genres. Additional helpful information can be found in a chronology of significant events in Black history and an excellent subject index. The easily accessible A to Z arrangement of this book makes it not only a useful reference but also an enjoyable book for browsing. Synopses of literary works are especially helpful; they enable the reader or researcher to discover information on authors' lives and the body of their work. Recommended for students in grades 7 through 12 and adults interested in Black literature.

Van Notten-Krepel, Eleonore. **Wallace Thurman's Harlem Renaissance**. Leiden: E. M. B. F. van Notten-Krepel, 1994. 365p. $72.61. ISBN 9-051-83692-9.

Wallace Thurman was only 30 years old when he died. He was extremely intelligent and valued his individuality. His residence, which he called "Niggerati Manor," was a home away from home and salon for his contemporaries. Van Notten-Krepel's well-researched book opens with a discussion of the "New Negro" and the forces that led to the movement. Thurman's family background is meticulously researched. Other areas of Thurman's life covered are his relationship with H. L. Mencken and his publishing of the literary quarterly *Fire!!* Details of Thurman's personal life, his failed marriage, and his painful illness and death from tuberculosis are all discussed at length. Van Notten-Krepel's work covers all facets of Thurman's life and provides insight and details not found elsewhere. Recommended for adults and students in grades 10 through 12.

Waldron, Edward C. **Walter White and the Harlem Renaissance**. Port Washington, NY: Kennikat Press, 1978. 186p. ISBN 0-8046-9197-5.

Walter White, a civil rights leader active in the National Association for the Advancement of Colored People (NAACP), also wrote two novels during the Harlem Renaissance: *The Fire in the Flint* and *Flight*. This thoroughly researched book delves into all aspects of White's life. However, the bulk of this study is devoted to analyses of White's novels. Waldron's analyses are objective, pointing out both strengths and weaknesses of White's works. This scholarly work is clear and straightforward. Recommended for adults and students in grades 10 through 12.

Wall, Cheryl A. **Women of the Harlem Renaissance**. Women of Letters Series. Bloomington, IN: Indiana State University Press, 1995. 246p. $32.35. ISBN 0-253-32908-6.

Wall has chosen Jessie Fauset, Nella Larsen, and Zora Neale Hurston as the subjects of her book. She opens with a discussion of race and gender, contrasting Alain Locke's perspective of the Renaissance and the "New Negro" with an essay by Marita Bonner, whose work was published by her daughter after her death. Bonner's work offers a female perspective of the Renaissance that sets the tone for Wall's profiles of her three subjects. Wall's work is straightforward and objective; her profile of Jessie Fauset, managing editor of *The Crisis*, cites flaws and weaknesses in Fauset's writing. Her discussion of Larsen includes the issue of color and the accusation of plagiarism that affected Larsen's writing career; she also discusses Larsen's use of the theme of the "tragic mulatto" in her work. Wall likens Hurston to a blues singer on the road. Unlike Larsen and Fauset, Hurston recorded language of real people. Hurston's association with her patron, Charlotte Mason, affected not only her work, but her daily life. Details of Hurston's agreement are provided. Wall also analyzes each writer's major works. Coverage is thorough, and the book's coverage of gender makes it an important resource. This book is written for adults, but is appropriate for students in grades 10 through 12.

Werner, Craig. **Black American Women Novelists: An Annotated Bibliography**. Magill Bibliographies Series. Metuchen, NJ: Scarecrow Press, 1989. 286p. $40.00. ISBN 0-8108-2787-5.

The introduction to this work contains approximately 250 citations to books, articles, and sources. The main section contains annotated citations of the works of 33 novelists, some of whom were Harlem Renaissance writers. In addition, Werner lists works of biography and general commentary about each author. The book is worth reading for Werner's introduction, alone, which is insightful and thorough. Designed for adult researchers, but student researchers in grades 10 through 12 will find it easy to use.

Witcover, Paul. **Zora Neale Hurston**. Black Americans of Achievement Series. New York: Chelsea House, 1991. 112p. $17.95. ISBN 0-7910-1129-1.

Clearly written, Witcover's book profiles Zora Neale Hurston's life and times. A large number of black-and-white photographs chronicle Hurston's private and professional life. Photos of Hurston and her contemporaries make this an excellent biography. A bibliography of the author's works and a chronology of important events in her life round out the book. This is an excellent example of biography written for students in grades 7 through 10.

Fig. 7.1.
W. E. B. Du Bois and publication staff in *The Crisis* office
(Schomburg Center, NYPL).

Periodicals

Many publications by and for African Americans appeared during the Harlem Renaissance. Among them were *Fire!!*, published by some of the writers themselves; *The Messenger*, originated by A. Philip Randolph; *The Crisis*, an NAACP publication conceived and edited by W. E. B. Du Bois and Jessie Fauset; and *Opportunity*, a publication of the National Urban League. *The Negro World*, a weekly newspaper, was published by Marcus Garvey's Universal Negro Improvement Association. *The Brownie's Book* was created by Jessie Fauset for children. These periodicals all published works of Harlem Renaissance writers, printed editorials on issues of the day, and due to their large circulation, influenced African American life and culture.

Learn more about these publications in these sources.

Bibliography

Kellner, Bruce, ed. **The Harlem Renaissance: A Historical Dictionary of the Era**. Westport, CT: Greenwood, 1984. 476p. $65.00. ISBN 0-313-23232-6.
With entries arranged by periodical title, one can easily find information on these publications in Kellner's dictionary. Entries are lengthy and offer information on the intent, content, publishers, and editors of the periodicals. Kellner's work is one of the most comprehensive works found on the Harlem Renaissance. His details on these publications are not readily found in many other sources. The dictionary format makes this book easy to access. Suitable for grades 7 through 12 and above.

Martin, Tony. **Literary Garveyism: Garvey, Black Arts and the Harlem Renaissance**. Dover, MA: Majority Press, 1983. 204p. $19.95. ISBN 0-912469-00-5.
Martin devotes a large portion of his work to Marcus Garvey's weekly newspaper, *The Negro World*. Published in Harlem beginning in 1918, the newspaper enjoyed worldwide circulation. Martin's premise is to disprove the notion that the publication was solely a political platform for Garvey. Several writers, including Zora Neale Hurston, Eric Walrond, and Arthur Schomburg, were published in *The Negro World*, as were reviews of music,

art, and drama. J. A. Rogers and Carter G. Woodson, both historians, were reviewed in the paper. Woodson, who created Black History Week in 1926, often had to publish his own works; a review in a paper with the circulation of *The Negro World* was vital to him. Excerpts of reviews are also included. Martin discusses Eric Walrond and Claude McKay, who both initially worked for the publication and later disassociated themselves with Garvey. In this thoroughly researched volume, Martin offers a wealth of information not found elsewhere. This book is written for adults, but is appropriate for students in grades 10 through 12.

Richardson, Janine. "Opportunity Knocks." **Cobblestone** 12, no. 2
    (February 1991): 6–9.
    Although this article is brief, it discusses the publications of the era. Several black-and-white photographs and a reproduction of the *Opportunity* logo are included. A list of foundations, organizations, and businesses that made financial contributions to the writers and artists of the Harlem Renaissance also appears. Written for younger readers, this article is also suitable for young adults.

Wintz, Cary D. **The Harlem Renaissance 1920–1940: Interpreta-**
    tion of an African American Literary Movement. 7 vols.
    New York: Garland, 1996. 3,160p. $552.00. ISBN 0-8153-2211-9.
    Wintz has compiled five volumes of essays, articles, lectures, speeches, reviews, and letters by writers of the era. The first five volumes consist of reprints from the periodicals published during the Harlem Renaissance, many of which appeared in *Opportunity* and *The Crisis*; the final two volumes consist of interpretations about the era by historians and other scholars. Arranged chronologically, the work includes contest awards, political commentary, literary analyses, and editorials by W. E. B. Du Bois, James Weldon Johnson, Alain Locke, and other writers of the era. This is an excellent source for those interested in the content of the era's publications. Recommended for students in grades 10 through 12 and above.

Quotations

Many famous people of the Harlem Renaissance are memorable because their messages are as valid today as they were when first spoken or written. Their words range from wise and witty to poignant and bitter, but they are always insightful. The following sources are listed for those who collect quotations or for those who wish to locate quotations of participants of the Harlem Renaissance. In their words, we can find a piece of history.

Bibliography

Bell, Janet Cheatham. **Famous Black Quotations**. New York: Time Warner, 1995. 144p. $7.99. ISBN 0-446-67150-9.

Quotations in this book are arranged by theme, some of which are "Struggle," "Identity," "Pride," and "Challenge." Several quotations by participants of the Harlem Renaissance can be found by accessing the index. Among those represented are W. E. B. Du Bois, 11 quotes; Langston Hughes, 3 quotes; Marcus Garvey, 8 quotes; and Zora Neale Hurston, 7 quotes. Browsers will also find quotations by Georgia Douglas Johnson, A. Philip Randolph, and Paul Robeson. This is not a reference book; rather, it is an enjoyable, hard-to-put-down volume containing quotations by many of the leading figures in the Harlem Renaissance. Recommended for grades 7 through 12 and above.

Diggs, Anita Doreen, comp. **Talking Drums: An African American Quote Collection**. New York: St. Martin's Press, 1995. 178p. $14.95. ISBN 0-312-11745-0.

Diggs has assembled more than 600 quotations into an arrangement of 76 themes. The quotations are then arranged chronologically within each theme. An alphabetical biographical list appears at the end of the book; Diggs lists field of endeavor here as well. The book features quotes by Langston Hughes on writing; Bill Robinson on performing, Zora Neale Hurston, Alain Locke, and Paul Robeson on America; Marian Anderson on character; Countee Cullen on death; and Hughes and Locke on Harlem. Recommended for grades 7 through 12 and above.

King, Anna. **Quotations in Black**. Westport, CT: Greenwood, 1981.
    320p. $45.00. ISBN 0-313-22128-6.
    Quotations in King's book are arranged chronologically by birth date;
they are also indexed by topic. There are even a few quotations on the
Harlem Renaissance, itself. Several quotations from those active in the
Harlem Renaissance can be found as well. This is an interesting source for
all ages.

Riley, Dorothy Winbush, ed. **My Soul Looks Back 'Less I Forget:
    A Collection of Quotations by People of Color**. Rev. ed. New
    York: HarperCollins, 1991. 512p. $14.00. ISBN 0-06-272057-0.
    The author, a schoolteacher who collected quotations, originally self-
published this book. It gained recognition by word of mouth. The table of
contents lists material by subject. There are two quotations on the Harlem
Renaissance by Alain Locke and Langston Hughes. An index lists speaker,
dates of birth and death, field of endeavor, and subject headings. The book
is easy to use and contains quotations of many who were part of the Harlem
Renaissance. It is suitable for readers in grades 7 through 12 and above.

Weinberg, Meyer, ed. **The World of W. E. B. Du Bois: A Quotation
    Sourcebook**. Westport, CT: Greenwood, 1992. 282p. $65.00.
    ISBN 0-313-28619-1.
    Weinberg has compiled more than 1,000 quotations attributed to Du
Bois and arranged them by topic. The 19 topics include "Women," "Literature," "Racism," and "Education"; the final chapter is devoted to material
that cannot be categorized. Each quotation is preceded by a title indicating
the subject of the complete quotation. Weinberg's index lists quotations by
decade and by subject. Recommended for adults and students in grades 7
through 12.

PART IV

Visual Arts

Fig. 9.1
Portrait of Langston Hughes by Richmond Barthé
(Schomburg Center, NYPL).

ART

Although much attention is given to writers of the Harlem Renaissance, several artists also gained wide recognition during this period. Like writers of the Renaissance, artists were financially supported by patrons and encouraged by prizes offered in *Opportunity* and other magazines. The Harmon Foundation was especially generous to African American artists. The Foundation regularly sponsored shows and exhibitions of African American art, some of which traveled to various cities across the United States. In addition to national exposure and recognition, artists could win hefty prizes for their work. Prize money enabled winners to work full-time at their endeavors. Many artists were also invited to salons where their works were exhibited for the other guests, many of whom were wealthy and influential gallery owners and philanthropists.

Painting, sculpture, collage, and various other media were used by Renaissance artists. Among noted artists of the period were Aaron Douglas, Sargent Johnson, Archibald Motley, and Augusta Savage.

Aaron Douglas

Aaron Douglas, known for his Egyptian themes and geometric shapes, was born in Kansas. He arrived in New York during the Harlem Renaissance and produced many illustrations for the African American publications of the day. He also produced posters for the Cotton Club and created murals and illustrations for books written by Countee Cullen, Langston Hughes, and Alain Locke.

Sargent Johnson

Sargent Johnson won several prizes from the Harmon Foundation for his sculptures. His work exhibits a strong African influence, and at least one of his works is derived from an African mask. Johnson's love of music is also evident in his work.

Archibald Motley

Archibald Motley was born in 1891 in New Orleans. He worked as a day laborer while studying at the Art Institute of Chicago. Among his early works are street scenes depicting the underside of society. However, Motley was an extraordinary talent, and his work demonstrates a variety of techniques and themes. He was also a winner of the Harmon Foundation award.

Augusta Savage

Augusta Savage was born in Florida. She began playing with the red Florida clay as a child, and as she grew older, her talent as a sculptor became evident. With the help of a benefactor, she went to New York to study and after overcoming many obstacles, she began to gain recognition. She sculpted busts of W. E. B. Du Bois, Marcus Garvey, and W. C. Handy.

These and other artists used African themes or city life as inspiration at some point in their careers. Although African themes were especially popular in the 1920s, benefiting from this popular trend was not the motivation of any of these artists. Each was an important voice of the Harlem Renaissance. Their creations were visual representations of the same ideas fostered by the writers of the Harlem Renaissance.

Read about and examine reprints of their work in the following sources.

Bibliography

Bearden, Romare, and Harry Henderson. **A History of African American Artists from 1792 to Present**. New York: Pantheon Books, 1993. 541p. $65.00. ISBN 0-394-57016-2.

Entries in this work, arranged chronologically, feature black-and-white and color prints of many Harlem Renaissance artists: W. H. Johnson, Aaron Douglas, Richmond Barthé, Archibald J. Motley, and Palmer C. Hayden. Profiles include details of personal lives and professional accomplishments. As an artist, Bearden is well qualified to discuss artists' techniques and styles; he does so clearly and thoroughly. Also of interest is the chapter entitled "Three Influential People." The authors discuss the impact on African American art of Alain Locke, known as the architect of the Harlem Renaissance; Charles Seifert, African American historian; and Mary Beattie Brady, director of the Harmon Foundation. Excellent for its historical perspective, details, and reproductions, this work also contains information not found elsewhere. This book is recommended for adults and students in grades 7 through 12.

Bontemps, Arna Alexander, ed. Jacqueline Fonvielle-Bontemps, dir. **Forever Free: Art by African American Women 1862–1980**. Alexandria, VA: Stevenson, 1980. 214p.

A catalog for a touring exhibition, this work provides information on female artists of the Harlem Renaissance not found in other sources. In addition to profiles of Augusta Savage and Meta Vaux Warrick Fuller are profiles of Nancy Prophet and Laura Wheeler Waring, both of whom painted during the Harlem Renaissance. Entries are arranged alphabetically, with birth and death dates, parents, occupation, education, awards, honors, medium, stylistic tendencies, and thematic concerns noted for each artist. A full-page color photograph of work shown at the exhibit is also included. Bibliographies, collections, and exhibits for each artist are listed in the appendix. Appropriate for adults and students in grades 7 through 12.

Driskell, David, David Levering Lewis, and Deborah Willis Ryan. **Harlem Renaissance: Art of Black America**. Introduction by Mary Schmidt Campbell. New York: Abrams, 1994. 200p. $14.98. ISBN 0-8109-8128-9.

Four artists of the Harlem Renaissance are profiled in this work: Meta Warrick Fuller, sculptor; William H. Johnson, painter; Aaron Douglas, painter: and Palmer C. Hayden, painter. The book features several photographs by James Van Der Zee. (See also chapter 11, "Photography.") Excellent selections of the artists' work appear in black-and-white and in color plates. This is an especially good resource because Fuller and Hayden, not as widely covered in other works, receive excellent, extensive treatment here. Driskell, Lewis, and Ryan are all well-respected writers on the African American experience. Recommended for adults and researchers in the fields of art and African American studies, this source can also be used by students in grades 10 through 12.

Estell, Kenneth, ed. "Fine and Applied Arts." In vol. 5 of **Reference Library of Black America**. Detroit, MI: Gale Research, 1993. 1,600p. $179.90. ISBN 0-685-49222-2.

Volume 5 of this work is introduced by an essay that focuses on the historical perspective of African American art. Included are several photographs of artwork, an index, and a bibliography at the end of the volume. In addition to a discussion of artists of the Harlem Renaissance, sections cover architecture and applied arts, a listing of exhibitions, and a listing of museums and galleries where the art of African Americans can be seen. Part of a five-volume set, this book is written for students in grades 7 through 12. The work was formerly titled *The Negro Almanac*, which was cited as outstanding by *Library Journal*.

Fine, Elsa Honig. **The Afro-American Artist: A Search for Identity**. New York: Holt, Rinehart & Winston, 1973. 310p. ISBN 0-030-91074-9.

In this chronologically arranged work, Fine focuses on the African American artist's search for identity, rather than on the art or the artist. The artists of the Harlem Renaissance era are seen as interpreters of life. However, Fine points out that this was debated by the intellectuals and the middle class of the era. She discusses the Harmon Foundation and profiles Palmer C. Hayden, Richmond Barthé, Archibald Motley, and Hale Woodruff. Fine also discusses Aaron Douglas as the only important artist of the period, a debatable point. Several black-and-white and color reproductions are included. This work is recommended for adults and students in grades 10 through 12.

Hedgepeth, Chester. **Twentieth-Century African-American Writers and Artists**. Chicago: American Library Association, 1991. 336p. $50.00. ISBN 0-8389-0534-X.

Nearly 250 profiles of artists, writers, and musicians make up this work. Each sketch is one to one-and-a-half pages long. Sketches include biographies, selected lists of primary and secondary works, and critiques. Sketches are informative, and the book is fairly comprehensive. Profiles of Harlem Renaissance artists include Augusta Savage, Henry Tanner, Richmond Barthé, and Aaron Douglas. This is a good starting point for research. Recommended for students in grades 10 through 12 and above.

Igoe, Lynn Moody, and James Igoe. **250 Years of Afro-American Art: An Annotated Bibliography**. New York: R. R. Bowker, 1987. Reprint. 1,291p. $180.00. ISBN 0-8357-8673-0.

Much more comprehensive than Hedgepeth's work, this book contains more than 25,000 citations on artists, artworks, and art history. It consists of a bibliography, artist bibliography, and subject bibliography. This is an excellent reference tool for those interested in African American artists and their work. Entries on artists of the Harlem Renaissance include Aaron Douglas, Augusta Savage, and Palmer C. Hayden. The book is designed for art researchers, but the "How to Use This Book" section is clear and thorough, making it usable by students in grades 10 through 12.

Kirschke, Amy. **Aaron Douglas: Art, Race, and the Harlem Renaissance**. Jackson, MS: University Press of Mississippi, 1995. 172p. $45.00. ISBN 0-87805-775-7.

Kirschke's book is a two-part study of Douglas. The first half of the work is a study of Douglas's early years in Topeka through his move to New York City in the 1920s. Kirschke discusses the effect on Douglas of W. E. B. Du Bois, Charles S. Johnson, and German artist Winold Reiss. She also examines Douglas's experiences with patronage, his art, and his intellectualism. Part 2 of the book focuses on the development of Douglas's style and his intense racial consciousness. Included are 82 illustrations, many of which were done by Douglas for magazine covers and posters. An extensive bibliography of primary and secondary sources rounds out the work. Recommended for students in grades 7 through 12 and above.

Lawrence, Jacob. **The Great Migration: An American Story**. Paintings by Jacob Lawrence with a Poem in Appreciation by Walter Dean Myers. New York: Museum of Modern Art, The Philips Collection, and HarperCollins, 1993. 60p. $22.00. ISBN 0-943044-20-0.

Although the text in this book is written for younger children, and Lawrence did not arrive in Harlem until 1930, this book is included for its subject matter. The Great Migration is one of the factors that contributed to the Harlem Renaissance. Lawrence's introduction explains the significance of the Great Migration in his life and in his work. A brilliant artist, Lawrence illustrates that the Great Migration was about movement. The book consists of 60 panels depicting the journey North during the 1920s. The language of the text is simple but powerful. Myers's poem is a moving addition to the work. Of interest to all ages for its subject matter and for Lawrence's exquisite art.

Porter, James A. **Modern Negro Art**. Moorland-Springarn Series. Washington, DC: Howard University Press, 1992. 276p. $24.95. ISBN 0-88258-163-5.

Originally published in 1943, Porter's work is an overview of African American art. Porter, himself, won a prize from the Harmon Foundation and was both an artist and art historian. The work is arranged chronologically, with chapter 6, "The New Negro Movement," covering the period of the Harlem Renaissance. Porter provides a discussion of conflicts among the intellectuals regarding art, literature, and music. He also discusses the effect of the Harmon Foundation on artists. Analyses of Laura Wheeler Waring's and Palmer C. Hayden's works are provided. Included also is a chronology and bibliography. Appropriate for adults and students in grades 10 through 12.

Powell, Richard J. **Homecoming: The Art and Life of William H. Johnson**. New York: National Museum of American Art and Rizzoli, 1993. 255p. $32.50. ISBN 0-8478-1421-1.

William H. Johnson, who arrived in Harlem in 1918, studied art at the School of the National Academy of Design. His career was just beginning during the Harlem Renaissance; however, he made important contributions even then and won the Harmon Gold Medal in 1929.

Arranged chronologically, chapters relating to the era are chapter 2, "Artistic Beginnings," and chapter 3, "First Successes." Plates of Johnson's work from each decade are interspersed with the text. Powell's work provides details of Johnson's life, including a brief meeting with Alain Locke and Langston Hughes. However, the real focus of this book is Johnson's work, which is beautifully reproduced. Recommended for grades 7 through 12 and above.

Reynolds, Gary A., and Beryl J. Wright. **Against the Odds: African American Artists and the Harmon Foundation**. Newark, NJ: The Newark Museum, 1989. 298p. $40.00. ISBN 0-932828-21-3.

Printed for an exhibition at the Newark Museum, this work presents not only several black-and-white and color reproductions, but also essays by experts such as Deborah Willis, David Driskell, Clement Alexander Price, and Richard J. Powell. The contributors all provide extensive information on the Harmon Foundation, which was so supportive of and important to artists of the Harlem Renaissance.

Mary Beattie Brady, director of the Harmon Foundation, is profiled. Her relationship with Alain Locke is discussed, as well as her fierce dedication to the Foundation and her interest in contemporary African American art. A section on photography is also included; the Foundation awarded prizes to photographers as well as to artists. Biographical sketches include reproductions of works shown at the exhibit. This is an outstanding source on artists of the Harlem Renaissance, particularly because of its inclusion of information and reproductions of works of lesser-known artists. Recommended for grades 10 through 12 and above.

Thomison, Dennis, comp. **The Black Artist in America: An Index to Reproductions**. Metuchen, NJ: Scarecrow Press, 1991. 456p. $47.50. ISBN 0-8108-2503-1.

Thomison's work covers several areas related to African American artists. In addition to listing artists, Thomison presents a history of recognition of African American artists, a catalog of each artist's works, a list of biographical and portrait sources, and an excellent bibliography. Harlem Renaissance artists are well represented. The history of recognition is especially appealing, and it can be used to trace an artist's recognition during the Harlem Renaissance. Recommended for researchers, but students in grades 10 through 12 can easily use this book, too.

Fig. 10.1.
Nina Mae McKinney and Paul Robeson
in *Sanders of the River* (Schomburg Center, NYPL).

Films and Film Companies

Black film companies were formed before and during the Harlem Renaissance. Clarence Brooks, Noble Johnson, and Clarence Muse were all actors who were involved with independent Black film companies. The owners acted, wrote, and directed films by and for African American audiences. Because these film companies were independent, they lacked the financial support of the large Hollywood studios and had to find backing for each project. Consequently, many Black film companies, such as the Lincoln Motion Picture Company, eventually went bankrupt.

Most notable among filmmakers was Oscar Micheaux. Micheaux began as a writer. He went to New York and formed his own film company so that he could produce films of his novels. He made many films during the Harlem Renaissance, one of which presented Paul Robeson in his first screen appearance. Micheaux's films were all low-budget because of a lack of funds. As a result, the films were not technically outstanding. Nevertheless, Micheaux succeeded in presenting films by and about African Americans. He was a tireless promoter of his works and took his films from city to city to have them shown. Although Paul Robeson has become very well known, other African Americans of the period made a living in films as well. Among them are Clarence Muse and Clarence Brooks. Both appeared in Hollywood productions as well as in independent films.

The list below contains references to films, filmmakers, and film companies.

Bibliography

Bogle, Donald. **Blacks in American Films and Television: An Encyclopedia**. Garland Reference Library of the Humanities Series. New York: Garland, 1988. 510p. $85.00. ISBN 08240-8715-1.

Arranged alphabetically by film, each entry provides a plot synopsis, characters, and Bogle's critical analysis, which is often very biting. Films related to the Harlem Renaissance include *Imitation of Life*, made toward the end of the era, and *Stormy Weather*, made after the era with many stars popular during the Harlem Renaissance. A section titled "Profiles" looks at and critiques the careers of approximately 100 African American performers and directors. Among the many stars of the 1920s and 1930s listed are Oscar Micheaux, Louise Beavers, Ethel Waters, Paul Robeson, and Bill Robinson. The book includes several black-and-white photographs. Bogle has written other reference works on African Americans in film and is considered an authority. This book is intended for adults, but it is also appropriate for students in grades 7 through 12.

————. **Brown Sugar: Eighty Years of America's Black Female Stars**. New York: Da Capo, 1990. 208p. $15.95. ISBN 0-306-80380-1.

Bogle explores the history of African American women in show business, with his premise being that each of his subjects is a diva with style. This premise is made clear in part 1 as Bogle profiles blues singer Ma Rainey, popular in the years preceding the Harlem Renaissance and the forerunner of all divas in later decades. Bogle's section devoted to the 1920s focuses on blues singers in general and Bessie Smith in particular. He provides biographical sketches of Florence Mills, Josephine Baker, Ethel Waters, and Nina Mae McKinney, all performers during the Harlem Renaissance. There is also an interesting section on chorus girls. Included are many black-and-white photographs and illustrations. Bogle's specialty is African Americans in film, and as with his other works, this one is well researched and clearly written. Information here, especially in the section on chorus girls, will not be found in other sources. Recommended for grades 7 through 12 and above.

————. **Toms, Coons, Mulattoes, Mammies, and Bucks: An Interpretive History of Blacks in American Films**. 3d. ed. New York: Continuum, 1994. Reprint. 400p. $19.95. ISBN 0-8264-0578-9.

Arranged chronologically, Bogle's work traces contributions of African Americans to film. As the title suggests, Bogle discusses the stereotypical roles relegated to African American performers in Hollywood. Only a small section of this work traces Black involvement in film during the 1920s. However, a lengthy section focuses on Oscar Micheaux. "Our Gang" comedies were made in the 1920s, and although they may not seem relevant to the Harlem Renaissance, Bogle's discussion of them is thought provoking. These stereotypes are what W. E. B. Du Bois and Alain Locke deplored and tried to eliminate. Also profiled are Bill Robinson, a dancer known as "The Mayor of Harlem," and Louise Beavers, who appeared with the Lincoln Players and the Lafayette Players in Harlem during the 1920s before moving on to Hollywood. Several black-and-white photographs complement the text. Excellent for its historical perspective, this book is recommended for adults and students in grades 7 through 12.

Cripps, Thomas. **Black Film as Genre**. Bloomington, IN: Indiana University Press, 1978. 192p. $54.80. ISBN 0-8357-7288-8.

Cripps has written a perceptive study of African American film that begins with an analysis of the history of African American films and includes an in-depth discussion of films from the Harlem Renaissance. Two films of the Renaissance era are discussed at length: *The Scar of Shame* and *St. Louis Blues*. Also included are a bibliography and filmography. Cripps has chosen to provide in-depth analysis for a select few films. His analyses are thorough and insightful. The book's arrangement is chronological and features black-and-white photographs of the films discussed. It is written for researchers and those interested in African American studies, but it is also suitable for students in grades 10 through 12 researching film.

Duberman, Martin. **Paul Robeson: A Biography**. New York: Alfred A. Knopf, 1988; reissued, 1996. 816p. $17.95. ISBN 1-56584-288-X.

Duberman's biography is excellent for many reasons. It is thoroughly researched, providing an intimate portrait of Paul Robeson as a public figure and as a man. It includes a detailed account of Robeson's experiences in film. The author's narrative style is highly readable, and the text is enhanced by more than 100 black-and-white photographs. The book also presents a social history of the times during which Robeson lived. Recommended for adults and students in grades 10 through 12.

Ehrlich, Scott. **Paul Robeson**. Black Americans of Achievement Series. New York: Chelsea House, 1988. 111p. $19.95. ISBN 1-555-46-608-7.

Ehrlich's book mixes biographical facts with career achievements. Paul Robeson was a man of many talents, and Ehrlich covers all facets of his life, including his appearances in film. The book features several black-and-white photographs and a chronology of achievements. This is part of an excellent series written for students in grades 7 through 10.

Kellner, Bruce, ed. **The Harlem Renaissance: A Historical Dictionary for the Era**. Westport, CT: Greenwood, 1984. 476p. $16.95. ISBN 0-416-01671-5.

Kellner's book is one of the few definitive books of the Harlem Renaissance. Kellner makes reference to the many film companies formed during the Harlem Renaissance on pages 250–51. Specific films produced by these companies are listed as well. Users can locate further information within the book for those films and film companies marked with an asterisk. (The asterisk denotes that the item has a separate entry.) The dictionary format makes this an easily accessible reference. The book is written for researchers and those interested in African American history and culture, specifically the Harlem Renaissance. It is a good source for students in grades 7 through 12.

Larsen, Rebecca. **Paul Robeson: Hero Before His Time**. New York: Franklin Watts, 1989. 158p. $15.33. ISBN 0-531-10779-5.

In this in-depth study of Paul Robeson's life, Larsen emphasizes equally his career and his political activities. Larsen, a reporter, includes excerpts from many documents, letters, and speeches. Her background in journalism is evident: Her writing is straightforward, and the book is well researched. She examines in detail Robeson's struggle against racism and his stand against injustice. Written especially for students in grades 7 through 10.

Leab, Daniel. **From Sambo to Superspade: The Black Experience in Motion Pictures**. New York: Houghton Mifflin, 1975. 301p. ISBN 0-395-19402-4.

Leab's premise is that one stereotype of African Americans in film was merely replaced by another. His work focuses on these stereotypes and on images of African Americans in general on the screen. Arranged chronologically, the chapters that relate to the Harlem Renaissance are chapter 4, "All Colored—But Not Very Different," and chapter 5, "Shufflin' Into Sound."

Leab discusses the Lincoln Motion Picture Company and presents summaries and critiques of films made by Lincoln and other companies. He discusses Oscar Micheaux as well. Chapter 5 focuses on talking motion pictures. Discussed are White and African American productions, including *Hallelujah*, an all-African American film made by King Vidor, a White director; and *The Jazz Singer* starring Al Jolson, a White performer who appeared in blackface for some of his musical numbers. Leab presents a clear view of obstacles faced by African Americans in front of and behind the camera. This work is currently out of print, but it is worth locating for the two chapters relating to the Harlem Renaissance and for information not found in other sources. Appropriate for adults and students in grades 10 through 12.

Sampson, Henry T. **Blacks in Black and White: A Source Book on Black Films**. Metuchen, NJ: Scarecrow Press, 1977. Reprint. 343p. $97.80. ISBN 0-8357-3594-X.
Sampson's work covers the time period 1910–50. Chapter 1 provides an overview and a chronological summary of significant events, Chapter 2 focuses on the Lincoln Motion Picture Company, and chapter 3 profiles Oscar Micheaux. Also included are film synopses and biographies. There is information on Charles Gilpin, Ralph Cooper, and Clarence Brooks, all working actors during the Harlem Renaissance. The time line in chapter 1 delineates many significant "firsts" in film during the Harlem Renaissance. Although it is neither critical nor interpretive, Sampson's work is an excellent source on film during the Harlem Renaissance, as much of the information in it is not found in other sources. Written for adults, Sampson's clear, straightforward writing makes this well-researched book appropriate for students in grades 10 through 12.

Photography

Photographs are an important part of history. They record the personal lives of people, but more important, they are a visual history. Many photographs recorded day-to-day life in Harlem, those active in the Harlem Renaissance, historical or significant events of the era, and celebrities. Famous Harlem Renaissance photographers include James Van Der Zee and Carl Van Vechten.

James Van Der Zee

One of the most widely known photographers of the Harlem Renaissance is James Van Der Zee. His work captures the essence of life in Harlem in the 1920s. Van Der Zee's photos all have an unmistakable mark of pride and dignity. He is a Harlem Renaissance figure whose work was "discovered" years after the demise of the Harlem Renaissance. Van Der Zee photographed many famous people, but the bulk of his work was done at his studio, photographing Harlem residents.

Carl Van Vechten

Although Carl Van Vechten was a man of many talents, his photography, like that of Van Der Zee, is unmistakably recognizable. Van Vechten's work focused on famous African Americans, and his collection of Harlem Renaissance portraits is stunning. Many of Van Vechten's portraits feature patterned backgrounds, making them highly individual. Long after the Harlem Renaissance, Van Vechten continued to photograph as many famous African Americans as he could.

Both of these men made major contributions to photography; however, it is important to look at the work of other photographers of the period as well.

Bibliography

Byrd, Rudolph P., ed. **Generations in Black and White: Photographs by Carl Van Vechten: From the James Weldon Johnson Memorial Collection**. Athens, GA: University of Georgia Press, 1993. 224p. $29.95. ISBN 0-8203-1558-3.

Most of the portraits in this collection are of Harlem Renaissance personalities. The introduction traces Carl Van Vechten's life and work and includes photos of him as well. Photos of W. E. B. Du Bois, James Weldon Johnson, W. C. Handy, Bill Robinson, Alain Locke, Aaron Douglas, and Paul Robeson are also featured. Van Vechten was an excellent photographer and his work is striking. Each photo is beautifully reproduced in Byrd's work. All photos are full page—the book is 8½" by 11"—and each facing page contains a biography of the subject. An excellent source for adults and students in grades 10 through 12.

Haskins, James. **James Van Der Zee: That Picture Takin' Man**. Trenton, NJ: Africa World Press, 1991. 256p. $45.00. ISBN 0-86543-260-0.

Haskins, author of more than 80 books, has won awards for his adult and young adult works. James Van Der Zee was born in Lennox, Massachusetts, and was taking pictures by the time he was in fifth grade. Many photos of Van Der Zee's family are included with many of Van Der Zee's other works. Haskins describes Van Der Zee's childhood, his move to New York, his first marriage, and the opening of his studio in Harlem in 1915. Later chapters trace the development of the Guarantee Photo Studio and Van Der Zee's later years. Van Der Zee, an excellent photographer, spent his entire life creating a photo history of Harlem and its people. However, as Haskins points out in a later chapter, Van Der Zee was "discovered" when he was 83 years old. An excellent source for students in grades 7 through 12 and above.

Siskind, Aaron. **Harlem: The 30s**. Petaluma, CA: Pomegranite Publications in cooperation with the National Museum of American Art, Smithsonian Institution. 32p. $12.95.

This book consists of 30 duotone photographs taken by Aaron Siskind during the 1930s. Many of the photographs show the bleaker side of everyday life in Harlem. These photographs offer a picture of the community at work, at play, during worship, and at mealtime. They provide an intimate look at homes, activities in church, and activities in the street. The photographs span the period leading to the decline of the Harlem Renaissance by the mid-1930s. All ages will appreciate Siskind's work in this book.

Willis-Thomas, Deborah. **Black Photographers, 1840–1940: An Illustrated Bio-Bibliography**. No. 401 of Garland Reference Library of the Humanities. New York: Garland, 1989. 500p. $95.00. ISBN 0-8240-9147-7.

Photographs in this volume range from wedding portraits to those of political leaders. Although it covers 100 years, it includes many photographs of the Harlem Renaissance. The author has collected biographical information as well as information on where and when the artists worked. Entries include dates, details of personal and professional life, location, processes used (a glossary of photographic processes is provided), principal subjects, collections, exhibitions, and bibliography. Listings indicate where the works are collected, and bibliographies outline published work by and about the artists. Lesser-known photographers of the Harlem Renaissance are included, among them James Latimer Allen, whose photographs of Claude

McKay, Countee Cullen, and Langston Hughes have been reproduced many times. Designed for adults, the book should be appealing to students in grades 10 through 12 as well.

————. **Van Der Zee: Photographer, 1886–1983**. New York: Abrams, 1993. 192p. $39.95. ISBN 0-8109-3923-1.

Opening with a discussion of Van Der Zee's work and the themes of family and self-worth—themes that are evident in every one of his photographs—Willis-Thomas compares and contrasts Van Der Zee's Harlem work with that of Aaron Siskind, whose work reflects desolation brought on by the Great Depression. Her writing is insightful and thoughtful. Roger C. Birt's biographical essay, "A Life in American Photography," details Van Der Zee's personal life. Included here are many family photographs. Birt also discusses techniques and props used in Van Der Zee's work. Photographs of Van Der Zee's studio are featured. The final section consists of plates of Van Der Zee's work, including portraits of the Renaissance Big Five, Harlem's basketball team; Marcus Garvey and Florence Mills; and a photograph of A'Lelia Walker's salon, The Dark Tower. The book is clearly written and the reproductions are excellent. Recommended for adults and students in grades 10 through 12.

Part V

The Performing Arts

Fig. 12.1.
Bessie Smith (Schomburg Center, NYPL).

Blues

The blues was and is not only a popular form of African American music; it is traditional American music. Its origins are believed to be rooted in slavery. Field songs, spirituals, and slave chants all played a part in the evolution of the blues.

In Harlem during the 1920s and 1930s, several blues singers appeared at clubs and cabarets. Interestingly, the most famous blues singers were women: Ida Cox, Alberta Hunter, Lil Green, Victoria Spivey, Ma Rainey, Mamie Smith, Bertha "Chippie" Hill, and Bessie Smith. Alberta Hunter and Victoria Spivey lived and worked in Harlem for years, even after the Harlem Renaissance; Hunter performed well into the 1980s. However, Bessie Smith is probably the most widely known blues singer, billed as "Empress of the Blues." W. C. Handy, composer of many blues songs, was also active during the Harlem Renaissance.

Read more about and listen to these great blues artists.

Bibliography

Albertson, Chris. **Bessie**. New York: Stein and Day, 1974. 253p. $8.95. ISBN 0-8128-1700-1.

Albertson has been involved with Bessie Smith's life and career for many years, having won Grammies for working on the Columbia Records reissues of her work. In fact, he is probably more responsible than any other writer for keeping her memory alive. Smith's life and career are fascinating; she was raucous, outspoken, and fun-loving. She was also one of the best blues singers ever and influenced many modern singers. Albertson captures her personality in this book. He also includes personal recollections of many who knew and worked with her. Thoroughly researched and well written, this book traces Smith's rise to fame, her personal ups and downs, and her tragic death in 1937. Several black-and-white photographs complete the volume. This book is written for adults, but is equally suitable for students in grades 7 through 12.

Albertson, Chris, comp. **Bessie Smith: Empress of the Blues**. New York: Macmillan, 1975. 143p. ISBN 0-028-70020-1.

Albertson, a widely known and respected jazz historian, wrote this book for younger readers. Although it is not available at this time, it is included here for several reasons. It is a beautifully designed book, the large black-and-white photographs of Smith are striking, and it is possible that copies of the book may be available in a public or school library. It is well worth looking for. The book begins with a biography of Bessie Smith's life. In addition to the photographs, there are reprints of ads from Columbia Records and the Lafayette Theatre, stills from the film *St. Louis Blues*, and several photographs taken by Carl Van Vechten. There are also several pages of music and lyrics from Smith's songs and a reprint of an original manuscript of the song "Pickpocket Blues." This is an excellent, well-written source for those who like the blues or who want to learn more about Bessie Smith. Appropriate for readers in grades 4 through 9.

Hammond, John, and Frank Walker, original prod. Michael Brooks, digital prod. **Bessie Smith, the Collection**. New York: Columbia Jazz Masterpieces, 1989. Audiocassette.

This newly reissued cassette features a selection of classic songs by Bessie Smith. Given the time period of these recordings, the sound quality is amazingly good. Smith's voice is clear, strong, and powerful. A highlight of this cassette is an excellent version of "Taint Nobody's Bizness If I Do," one of her more widely known songs, recorded in New York in 1923. Other songs worth listening to are "Downhearted Blues," written by Alberta Hunter, and "St. Louis Blues," written by W. C. Handy. Bessie Smith was one of the most popular personalities during the Harlem Renaissance; this cassette will introduce new listeners to her music and delight those who are already her fans. Recommended for blues lovers and for those who wish to know what popular music Harlemites were listening to during the Renaissance.

Handy, W. C. **Father of the Blues: An Autobiography**. Roots of Jazz Series. New York: Da Capo, 1985. Reprint. 317p. $37.50. ISBN 0-306-76241-2.

W. C. Handy's autobiography is a lively narrative detailing his life and relationships with family, friends, and associates. Handy recounts incidents of prejudice as a child and as a composer trying to sell and record his music. He discusses the popularity of the blues during the Harlem Renaissance. Handy also provides a chronology of his compositions, arrangements, and books. Full of anecdotes and dialogue, this is an appealing source. Recommended for adults and students in grades 7 through 12.

Harrison, Daphne Duval. **Black Pearls: Blues Queens of the 1920s**. New Brunswick, NJ: Rutgers University Press, 1988. 225p. $13.95. ISBN 0-8135-1280-8.

More than a selection of profiles of blues singers, Harrison's work is a social history of the era as well. She discusses the effects of the Great Migration on African American women's lives and on the blues. Harrison also details the impact of the birth of the recording industry and the Theatre Owner's Booking Association on these women and their music. The author delves into the lives of female blues singers. Edith Wilson, Alberta Hunter, Victoria Spivey, and Sippie Wallace are all discussed at length. Styles and lyrics are also examined. Of particular interest are the chapters on Hunter and Wilson, in which Harrison details their involvement in and contributions to the Harlem Renaissance. In an appendix, "Other Blues Singers," Harrison provides one- to two-page profiles of lesser-known blues singers of the era. Selected titles, glossary, and bibliography are also included, as are black-and-white photographs.

Although only a small section of this work may seem relevant to the Harlem Renaissance, it is an important source for its discussion of the role of African American women in society or at least in one aspect of it, during the era. Recommended for students in grades 10 through 12 and adults.

Herzhaft, Gerard. **Encyclopedia of the Blues**. Translated by Brigette Debord. Fayetteville, AR: University of Arkansas Press, 1992. 488p. $18.95. ISBN 1-55728-253-6.

This volume is an excellent source of information on the blues. Each of the women mentioned in the opening of this chapter is profiled in a section titled "Classic Blues Singers of the Twenties." Individual listings profile Bessie Smith, Victoria Spivey, and Ma Rainey, all performers during the Harlem Renaissance. An extensive bibliography and discographies are included. "Blues Standards" lists more than 300 famous blues songs and gives details of each song's origin and the most original interpretation, along with several humorous anecdotes. The encyclopedia format makes this an easy-to-use, enjoyable source for blues lovers of all ages.

Shaw, Arnold. **Black Popular Music in America from the Spirituals, Minstrals, and Ragtime to Soul, Disco and Hip Hop**. New York: Schirmer Books, 1986. 386p. $21.95. ISBN 0-02872-310-4.

Shaw's chapter 5, "Singin' the Blues," is an excellent source of information not only on the great blues singers like Ma Rainey, Bessie Smith, and Mamie Smith, but also on the origins of the blues. At the end of the chapter, a section called "The White Synthesis" analyzes the Black–White connection during the Harlem Renaissance. The book includes bibliographies and discographies, along with a variety of black-and-white photos. It is also a good source of social history. Shaw writes in a conversational and engaging style, making this a delightful source for students in grades 10 through 12.

Tracey, Steven. **Langston Hughes and the Blues**. Urbana, IL: University of Illinois Press, 1988. 306p. $29.95. ISBN 0-252-01457-X.

Tracey, who holds a Ph.D. in English and is also a blues performer, opens his work with a discussion of folklore and its place in the literature of the Harlem Renaissance. After discussing the origin of the blues, Tracey demonstrates Hughes's use of blues structures, themes, and imagery in specific poems. Tracey's discussion of the Harlem Renaissance focuses on Zora Neale Hurston and Sterling Brown, both folklorists and contemporaries of Hughes. Tracey also analyzes Alain Locke's, W. E. B. Du Bois's and James Weldon Johnson's conflicting views on folklore; the need for racial pride on one hand contradicted elitist views, concern over the proper African American image, and preference for White values on the other. Tracey provides thorough background on the blues, detailed analyses of Hughes's poems, and linkages between the two. Nonmusicians may become lost in some of the musical discussions; however, Tracey's work is unique and authoritative. Included are a biography and discography. Recommended for adults and students in grades 10 through 12.

Fig. 13.1.
Duke Ellington (Schomburg Center, NYPL).

Jazz

Jazz is traditional African American music native to the United States. New Orleans is considered to be the birthplace of jazz, and the varied cultures of the city are reflected in elements of early jazz. Its origins, like those of the blues, can be traced to field hollers, chants, and rhythms of slaves. Over time, some European elements were added. Spanish rhythms and elements of the French quadrille are evident in early jazz.

Jazz has evolved tremendously over the years. The period of the Harlem Renaissance was a time when jazz reached its peak not only in Harlem, but all across America. The period of the 1920s was known as "The Jazz Age"; jazz swept the country.

Many jazz musicians achieved fame during the Harlem Renaissance. They are too numerous to mention here, but among the most notable are Louis Armstrong, Duke Ellington, Fletcher Henderson, and Fats Waller.

Louis Armstrong

New Orleans, the birthplace of jazz, is also the birthplace of Louis "Satchmo" Armstrong. Armstrong was reportedly born in 1900, only 40 years after the abolition of slavery. Many believe Armstrong did more to modernize jazz than anyone else. He was one of the first musicians known to perform solo on his recordings, a concept he developed with his band. He was also the first person to do "scat" singing, which entails using the voice to imitate the sound of an instrument. His work brought recognition and innovation to this form of music.

Duke Ellington

One of the most famous bandleaders of the Harlem Renaissance was Duke Ellington, whose orchestra played regularly at the Cotton Club. In fact, his orchestra was the house band from 1928 until 1931, when Cab Calloway took over. His music was broadcast live from the club across the country. He scored his own music and developed a unique sound. Ellington and Armstrong are considered to be the major influences in the modernization of early jazz. Many believe that all music played today is in some way related to what Louis and Duke did for jazz.

Fletcher Henderson

Fletcher Henderson also gained fame by playing at the Cotton Club. He started in New York, however, by accompanying blues singers. He also led a dance band at Roseland, a popular dance hall in New York City. In 1924, Louis Armstrong joined Henderson's band in New York. This proved to be a milestone event as Henderson's band went on to become the first full band to play jazz. Henderson also developed a reputation as an excellent arranger for other bands during the 1930s.

Fats Waller

Fats Waller worked in Harlem playing at rent parties and cabarets before making a name for himself. He was unique because his sense of humor was part of his music. It wasn't long before he began playing in nightclubs. He recorded novelty songs like "Your Feet's Too Big" and "Your Socks Don't Match." Two of his songs have become standards, "Honeysuckle Rose" and "Ain't Misbehavin'." Waller was an original; however, beneath all the fun, he was a serious musician.

Other jazz musicians popular in Harlem during the Renaissance were Willie "the Lion" Smith and James P. Johnson, both great stride piano players. Stride piano playing was considered a Harlem creation. It evolved from ragtime and was believed to have originated at rent parties—parties at which Johnson and Smith worked frequently. Their classical training contributed to the style they originated, a style that has influenced many modern musicians. (See also chapter 19, "Cotton Club," and chapter 20, "Entertainers," for information on other musicians.)

Use these sources to read about and listen to these famous jazz artists.

Bibliography

Avakian, George, prod. **The Louis Armstrong Story**. New York: Columbia Masterworks, 1978. Audiocassettes; reissue.

This four-volume set includes recordings from the years 1925–31. Classics include "Muskrat Ramble," "Stardust," and "St. James Infirmary." The music is lively. The sound quality varies from cut to cut. It is an excellent choice for those who wish to hear the music as it was originally recorded during the Harlem Renaissance. Compare this set with the "Louis Armstrong and King Oliver" entry to see how Armstrong evolved as a musician from sideman to band leader.

Balliett, Whitney. **American Musicians: Fifty-Six Portraits in Jazz**. New York: Oxford University Press, 1986. 415p. $35.00. ISBN 0-19-505410-5.

Balliett, a highly regarded writer on jazz, has compiled a series of jazz profiles originally written for *The New Yorker*. This selection stands out for many reasons: Balliett has profiled lesser-known musicians, the profiles give readers an in-depth glimpse of the musicians' personal and professional lives, and finally, the book serves as an oral history of jazz. Musicians popular during the Harlem Renaissance included in Balliett's work are Jelly Roll Morton, Henry "Red" Allen, Duke Ellington, and Fats Waller. In addition, many other profiles contain reminiscences of Renaissance-era musicians. Balliett's work is significant not only for its biographical content but also for its historical perspective. Highly recommended for jazz fans and others interested in the evolution of the history of jazz. Appropriate for students in grades 10 through 12 and adults.

Collier, James Lincoln. **Duke Ellington**. New York: Oxford University Press, 1987. 340p. $30.00. ISBN 0-19-503770-7.

Collier's in-depth biography of Duke Ellington traces events in his personal and professional life and highlights his musical achievements. Collier emphasizes Ellington's earlier years, making this an excellent source for those researching Ellington's Harlem Renaissance years. An entire chapter is devoted to Ellington's arrival in New York in 1923, and another is devoted to his years at the Cotton Club. Collier presents specific information about band members: hirings, firings, and personal and professional qualities. Collier also discusses previous Ellington biographies and incorporates oral histories of many who knew Ellington. As a result, the book contains many anecdotes and information not found in other Ellington biographies.

Collier also discusses Ellington's music. As a musician himself, Collier is knowledgeable; his discussions may seem at times esoteric to nonmusicians, but this work is well worth reading. A section of black-and-white photographs rounds out the book. Recommended for adults and students in grades 10 through 12.

———. **The Great Jazz Artists**. Monoprints by Robert Andrew Parker. New York: Four Winds Press, 1977. $7.95. ISBN 0-590-07493-8.

Collier is widely known for his young adult historical fiction that he writes with his brother. The Collier brothers have an excellent reputation for writing books that reflect thorough, in-depth research. This book is no exception, and the research on jazz artists makes it fascinating reading. Various artists are profiled. Each profile is from 6 to 12 pages long and includes a discography and bibliography. Of special interest to researchers of the Harlem Renaissance are chapters on Louis Armstrong, Duke Ellington, and Fletcher Henderson. This book is not currently in print, but because it is difficult to find information and discographies of Fletcher Henderson, it is included here. Written for students in grades 7 through 12.

———. **Louis Armstrong: An American Genius**. New York: Oxford University Press, 1983. 383p. $35.00. ISBN 0-19-503377-9.

Collier has written several books on jazz. All are painstakingly researched, and this one is no exception. In it, Collier sets out to separate fact from fiction in Louis Armstrong's life, including his July 4, 1900, birth date and the reasons for commercialism in his music in later years. The result is an insightful portrait of one of America's most influential musicians. Of special interest to Harlem Renaissance buffs are chapters 10 through 15. Also worth perusing are the black-and-white photographs and discography. Although written for adults, this book is recommended for students in grades 10 through 12 as well.

————. **The Making of Jazz**. New York: Houghton Mifflin, 1978. 543p. $15.00. ISBN 0-395-26286-0.

In this book, Collier focuses on the origins of jazz and those who helped shape it. A small section of this work relates to musicians popular during the Harlem Renaissance: Louis Armstrong, Bessie Smith, and Fletcher Henderson are discussed in depth. Collier also discusses stride piano, also known as Harlem stride piano. James P. Johnson, Willie "the Lion" Smith, and Fats Waller, all stride piano players, are profiled. Information on Fletcher Henderson and stride piano players, difficult to locate, is found here. Collier's writing is clear and authoritative as he presents personal and professional highlights of those profiled. Several black-and-white photographs, a discography, and a bibliography are included. Appropriate for adults and students in grades 10 through 12.

Estell, Kenneth, ed. "Jazz and Blues." In vol. 4 of **Reference Library of Black America**. Detroit, MI: Gale Research, 1993. 1,600p. $179.90. ISBN 0-685-49222-2.

Chapter 22 in Estell's work includes sections on early recordings, bandleaders, composers, singers, and instrumentalists. Many musicians of the Harlem Renaissance are profiled, with photographs included. This book has been highly acclaimed by *Library Journal*. A bibliography at the end of the book lists many titles related to jazz musicians of the period. Each of the volumes in the five-volume almanac contains a complete index, making volume 4 easy to use. Written for students in grades 7 through 12.

Feather, Leonard. **The Encyclopedia of Jazz**. New York: Da Capo, 1984. Reprint. 527p. $19.95. ISBN 0-306-80214-7.

This well-known, time-honored reference on jazz is arranged alphabetically and contains more than 200 black-and-white photographs. It also includes a historical survey of jazz and a chronology that lists many "firsts" that occurred during the Harlem Renaissance years. Other sections—"The Anatomy of Jazz" and "Jazz in American Society"—trace the history of jazz in this country. Entries include nicknames, instrument played, dates of birth and death, place of birth, career achievements, recordings, and addresses of performers. This book is written for jazz aficionados, but is useful for researchers and fans of all ages.

Floyd, Samuel A., Jr. **The Power of Black Music**. New York: Oxford University Press, 1995. 316p. $30.00. ISBN 0-19-508235-4.

Floyd's work is arranged chronologically. Chapter 5, "The Negro Renaissance: Harlem and Chicago Flowerings," begins with a discussion of African American music and nationalist movements, particularly Marcus Garvey's movement. Other topics presented are big bands, classic blues singers, and stride piano playing. Floyd also explains the conflict between what he refers to as high art and low art during the Harlem Renaissance. Floyd provides historical perspective, analyzes recordings, and describes the effects of music on the Harlem Renaissance and vice versa. Appendixes cite printed works, sound recordings, and films and videotapes. The index is excellent. Floyd's work is scholarly, but his insightful discussion of the relationship between the Harlem Renaissance and music is informative and thought provoking. Recommended for students in grades 10 through 12 and adults.

Floyd, Samuel, Jr., and Marsha J. Reisser. **Black Music Biography: An Annotated Bibliography**. White Plains, NY: Kraus International, 1987. 302p. ISBN 0-527-30158-2.

The authors have compiled an annotated bibliography of biographies of several Harlem Renaissance-era musicians. Among them are Louis Armstrong, Eubie Blake, Cab Calloway, Duke Ellington, and Fats Waller. Each work is annotated with reviews and a discography. This book is not available from the publisher at this time and many sources listed in it may be out of print. The authors, however, suggest that their work could be used as a series of vignettes because annotations provide highlights of professional and personal lives. Annotations read like short narratives. The introduction lists performers in chronological order, making it easy to single out Harlem Renaissance artists. Recommended for adults and students in grades 10 through 12.

Frankl, Ron. **Duke Ellington**. Black Americans of Achievement Series. New York: Chelsea House, 1988. 112p. $17.95. ISBN 1-55546-584-6.

Frankl's book provides details of Duke Ellington's personal life and career. Included in this book are many black-and-white photographs, publicity stills, and advertisements. Chapters relating to the Harlem Renaissance are "Jump for Joy," "Let Me Off in Harlem," and "Black and Tan Fantasy." The book is detailed and written in a straightforward manner. Included are a chronology and discography. It is part of an excellent series written for students in grades 7 through 10.

Gammond, Peter, ed. **Duke Ellington: His Life and His Music**. Roots of Jazz Series. New York: Da Capo, 1977. Reprint. 256p. $29.50. ISBN 0-306-70874-4.

Gammond's work is a collection of essays on various aspects of Duke Ellington. The book is arranged in four sections: "The Man," "The Music," "The Musicians," and "Record Guide." Section 1 consists of a profile by Stanley Dance, who knew Ellington, as well as profiles by three other musicians. Section 2 consists of chronologically arranged essays on Ellington's recordings. The 1920s and 1930s are well covered. Section 3 contains profiles on Ellington's band members. Each profile includes a critique of style and recording dates. Section 4 is a discography. Gammond has compiled an interesting mix of essays on Ellington. This work is a valuable complement to other biographies on Ellington listed in this section. Appropriate for adults and students in grades 10 through 12.

Gottlieb, Robert, ed. **Reading Jazz: A Gathering of Autobiography, Reportage, and Criticism from 1919 to Now**. New York: Pantheon Books, 1996. 1,088p. $40.00. ISBN 0-679-4425-1-0.

More than 150 excerpts from books and periodicals make up this work, organized in three sections: autobiography, reportage, and criticism. Gottlieb has used excellent judgment in choosing titles for inclusion. The autobiography section consists of excerpts of hard-to-find books, including Calloway's autobiography. Not all excerpts pertain to musicians of the Harlem Renaissance, but the book is well worth reading for those that do. This book is written for adults, but is appropriate for students in grades 10 through 12.

Harrison, Max, Charles Fox, and Eric Thacker. **Ragtime to Swing**. Vol. 1 of The Essential Jazz Records. No. 12 of the Discographies Series. Westport, CT: Greenwood, 1984. 595p. $69.50. ISBN 0-313-24674-2.

The authors, working jazz critics from Great Britain, have selected more than 250 discs that best represent the jazz music of the period. Even though the largest section of the book deals with the 1930s, there is a good representation of discs covering the 1920s as well. Each entry is detailed; in addition to title, the authors describe each track in detail and provide a rather lengthy commentary. This is an excellent discography of the Harlem Renaissance era. It is a good source for jazz lovers. In addition, students in grades 10 through 12 who wish to learn more about music of the 1920s and 1930s will find it informative and easy to read.

Haskins, James. "Black Renaissance." In **Black Music in America: A History Through Its People.** New York: HarperCollins, 1987. 224p. $15.89. ISBN 0-690-04462-3.

This volume covers a variety of music, but chapter 5 will be of the most interest as it offers an overview and provides some background on the Cotton Club and other establishments that featured jazz during the Harlem Renaissance. Among those profiled is Duke Ellington. Profiles include personal and career milestones, along with a discography and bibliography. Black-and-white photographs enhance the text. Haskins is a prolific writer on the African American experience. His books are geared to students in grades 7 through 12.

Keepnews, Orrin, prod. **Louis Armstrong and King Oliver**. Musical Heritage Society, 1993. Audiocassette, reissue. $9.95.

There are other Louis Armstrong reissues, but this tape is notable for two rare cuts, "Zulu's Ball," and "Working Man Blues." All of side 1 and five cuts from side 2 are recordings of King Oliver's Creole jazz Band with Armstrong as a sideman on cornet. The remaining cuts on side 2 are by Louis Armstrong and his Red Onion Jazz Babies. These selections were cut in New York City in 1924. There is a special treat on the last three selections: vocals by Alberta Hunter. The sound quality of this audiocassette varies from cut to cut. Nevertheless, this is a fine example of popular music from the 1920s.

Kernfeld, Barry, ed. **The New Grove Dictionary of Jazz**. New York: Grove's Dictionaries of Music, 1988. 1,400p. $350.00. ISBN 0-935859-39-X.

This source, consisting of 4,500 entries, contains a wide range of information, some of it related to the Harlem Renaissance. In the section on record companies, for example, there is information on Black Swan Records, the first Black-owned record company, and which was a popular label during the Harlem Renaissance. In addition, discographies of Duke Ellington, Cab Calloway, Fletcher Henderson, and other jazz artists of the era list a range of titles. Grove is a respected publisher of music references; this one will be easy for music buffs of all ages to use.

Peretti, Burton W. **The Creation of Jazz: Music, Race, and Culture**. Urbana, IL: University of Illinois Press, 1992. 282p. $29.95. ISBN 0-252-01708-0.

Several chapters in this history of jazz relate to the Harlem Renaissance. Peretti explains chronologically how the Great Migration—the movement of many African Americans from rural, southern towns to large northern cities—influenced the development of jazz. Peretti even uses a chart to trace the migration patterns of musicians during the 1920s. Rather than focus on specific musicians, Peretti's book focuses on jazz, itself. This is an appealing source for those interested in the history of jazz. This book is written for adults, but students in grades 10 through 12 may find it useful as well.

Shaw, Arnold. **The Jazz Age: Popular Music in the 1920s**. New
   York: Oxford University Press, 1987. Reprint. 368p. $27.95.
   ISBN 0-19-503891-6.
   Shaw covers all music popular in the 1920s; however, of interest to
Harlem Renaissance researchers are parts 1 and 2. Part 1, "The Jazz Age,"
provides information on flappers and gangsters and defines terms used at
the time. Louis Armstrong and King Oliver are also discussed. Part 2, "The
Harlem Renaissance," covers Duke Ellington, the blues, and the evolution
of ragtime into stride piano. One chapter looks at *Shuffle Along* and its
impact on Broadway. Shaw discusses speakeasies and cabarets, adding a
social history facet to the topic. Shaw's style is lively, and his research is
thorough. Many anecdotes make this book fun to read, as well as informative. A bibliography, a discography of performers and composers, a list of top
100 songs, and an index complete the book. Recommended for adults and
students in grades 7 through 12.

Smith, Willie the Lion. With George Hoefer. **Music on My Mind: The
   Memoirs of an American Pianist**. New York: Da Capo, 1975.
   318p. ISBN 0-306-70684-9.
   Smith's autobiography is entertaining, thanks to his lively narrative.
Smith writes of his life, his music, and his associations with Fats Waller, James
P. Johnson, and Luckey Roberts, all stride piano players in Harlem during the
Renaissance. He also writes of Mamie Smith, Florence Mills, and many other
musicians popular during the era. Smith could be intimidating, but he was also
very humorous. Much of his autobiography covers the Harlem Renaissance. The
book is not in print at this time, but it is worth tracking down as it contains a
wealth of information on Harlem; it is an excellent source of social history, as
well as a wonderfully readable autobiography. Recommended for adults and
students in grades 10 through 12.

Southern, Eileen. **The Music of Black Americans: A History**. 3d
   ed. New York: W. W. Norton, 1997. 678p. $24.50. ISBN 0-393-
   03843-2.
   Southern's work traces the history of African American music from
1619. Part 4, "Lift Ev'ry Voice, 1920–," is devoted for the most part to the
music of the Harlem Renaissance. Not only does Southern profile all major
musicians of the period, she discusses lesser-known musicians and composers. For example, she provides information on Charles Luckeyth "Luckey"
Roberts, a stride piano player often overlooked or mentioned only in passing.
In addition, Southern discusses Black Swan Record Company, an African
American-owned company, and Edmond's Cellar, a small nightclub popular
in Harlem during the Renaissance. Her work is narrative in form, but the
index provides easy access. Recommended for adults and students in grades
7 through 12.

Tanenhaus, Sam. **Louis Armstrong**. Black Americans of Achievement Series. New York: Chelsea House, 1989. 112p. $17.95.
   ISBN 1-55546-571-4.
   Louis Armstrong was instrumental in establishing jazz as the first
truly American music. This biography traces his birth in New Orleans, his
difficult childhood, his initial success as a musician, and his ultimate
worldwide fame. Included are several black-and-white photographs, as well
as a selective discography, chronology, and listing of books for further
reading. Easily readable, this work provides many details of Louis Armstrong's professional achievements and personal life. Written for students
in grades 7 through 12.

Tucker, Mark. **Ellington: The Early Years**. Music in American Life
Series. Urbana, IL: University of Illinois Press, 1990. 348p.
$34.95. ISBN 0-252-01425-1.

Many biographies have been written about Duke Ellington, but this
one focuses exclusively on Ellington's professional life up to and including
1927, before he went on to the Cotton Club. Tucker devotes part 1 of this
work to Ellington's early years in Washington, D.C., his birthplace. Part 2
begins in 1923, when Ellington and his band arrive in New York, during the
Harlem Renaissance. Also described are the band's first recordings and
Ellington's early compositions. Tucker discusses nightlife and stride piano
players, as well as the impact of Harlem on Ellington. Several black-and-
white photographs, excerpts of musical compositions, and a chronological
discography are other features of the book. A bibliography, general index,
and index of compositions, recordings, and arrangements round out the
volume. This book is written for adults, but is also appropriate for students
in grades 10 through 12.

Tucker, Mark, ed. **The Duke Ellington Reader**. New York: Oxford
University Press, 1993. 536p. $30.00. ISBN 0-19-505410-5.

Tucker has compiled into one volume more than 100 interviews,
essays, reviews, and memoirs, including writings by Duke Ellington himself.
As a major force in American music, Ellington deserves the recognition and
coverage Tucker has provided in this work. The selections are varied and
the reader learns about all facets of Ellington's personal and professional
life. Parts 1 and 2 cover Ellington's early life and his years at the Cotton
Club. Tucker's work is written for music lovers and Ellington devotees, but
many selections will be of interest to general readers. Appropriate for adults
and students in grades 10 through 12.

Waller, Maurice, and Anthony Calabrese. **Fats Waller**. Foreword by
Michael Lipskin. New York: Schirmer Books, 1977. ISBN 0028-
72730-4.

Fats Waller was a popular entertainer who performed at various clubs
and cabarets during the Harlem Renaissance. He was known for his humor
and for his talent as a stride piano player. Although this book is out of print,
it is worth looking for. Written by Waller's son, it is a well-documented
account of Waller's private and public life. Waller recalls incidents in family
life and his father's encounters with racism and relationships with other
entertainers. The book also discusses Waller's music at length. This book is
written for adults, but is also appropriate for students in grades 10 through
12.

Woog, Adam. **The Importance of Duke Ellington**. The Importance
of Series. San Diego, CA: Lucent Books, 1996. 112p. $18.31.
ISBN 1-56006-073-5.

Part of a series written for young adults, Woog's work opens with a
chronology of Duke Ellington's life. Throughout the text, Woog excerpts
passages from other works on Ellington. Chapters 3 through 5 deal with the
Harlem Renaissance era. Interesting anecdotes, such as how Ellington came
to work at the Cotton Club and Ellington's excuse for arriving late for a
concert make this book thoroughly enjoyable. Several black-and-white photographs and a bibliography are included. Sidebar quotations from primary
and secondary sources are informative and insightful as well. Although
written for students in grades 7 through 10, this work is an appealing and
well-written source for Ellington fans and readers of all ages.

Wright, Laurie. **"Fats" in Fact**. Essex, England: Storyville, 1992. 552p. ISBN 0-902391-14-3.

Wright has compiled a comprehensive work on Fats Waller. As the title suggests, Wright set out to separate fact from fiction surrounding Waller's life. The book opens with an excerpt in Waller's own words. Wright then presents a biography and discography. Notes, information, and reminiscences are interspersed with the discography, making this book more interesting than most. Wright has included a section of piano rolls made by Waller and a section called "The Miscellaneous Fats Waller." This is also full of bits of information about Fats. Ernie Anderson, who promoted Fats Waller's Carnegie Hall concert, and Courtney Williams, a former band member, each wrote memoirs of their experiences with Waller. Several black-and-white photographs are included, as well as a "Scrapbook" of many more photos. There are indexes of people and places, tune titles, record catalogs, and even a section of copyrights. This well-researched book is an excellent source on Fats Waller. Appropriate for adults and students in grades 10 through 12.

Classical and Concert Music

During the Harlem Renaissance, many classically trained singers and musicians gained prominence. Among the most widely known are Marian Anderson, Roland Hayes, and William Grant Still. These artists accomplished many "firsts" for African Americans in the field of classical music. Paul Robeson also won acclaim as a concert singer.

Marian Anderson

Marian Anderson grew up in Philadelphia, where she sang in a church choir. Members of her church were so impressed with her abilities that they collected money so that she could study voice. Anderson had a brilliant career, but she had to overcome bigotry and initial failure as a concert singer. During the Harlem Renaissance, Anderson won a singing competition, which finally opened the door to success first in Europe and later in the United States. Some years after the Renaissance, Anderson was still a victim of bigotry. The Daughters of the American Revolution prevented her from performing at Constitution Hall in Washington, D.C. On learning about this, First Lady Eleanor Roosevelt arranged to have Anderson sing on the steps of the Lincoln Memorial instead.

Roland Hayes

Roland Hayes was born in Georgia in 1887. His parents were former slaves. Although he lived in poverty, Hayes, encouraged by his mother, managed to study at night and eventually studied music at Fisk University in Tennessee. Like Marian Anderson, Hayes found more opportunities in Europe. He toured the Continent, then returned to the United States in 1923, a renowned and respected concert artist. He sang professionally until he was 75 years old.

Paul Robeson

Paul Robeson was multitalented. He was a brilliant student at Rutgers University and an excellent athlete as well. He financed his law school studies by playing professional football. He also won acclaim as an actor and concert singer during the Harlem Renaissance. However, he was controversial in his political beliefs. Although this caused problems with the United States government, Robeson did not relent in his pursuit of equality. (See also chapter 10, "Film and Film Companies," and chapter 16, "Theatre.")

William Grant Still

William Grant Still was raised in a musical family. He was hired as an oboist for the show *Shuffle Along*. However, he soon switched to classical music and is responsible for many classical compositions. During his career, Still won several awards, including a Harmon Foundation award. He accomplished many "firsts" for African Americans in the field of classical music.

Read more about these musicians and others, such as Eva Jessye and John Rosamond Johnson, in the following references.

Bibliography

Abdul, Raoul. **Blacks in Classical Music: A Personal History**. New York: Dodd, Mead, 1977. 253p. $8.95. ISBN 0-396-07394-8.

Abdul's subjects are listed according to musical endeavor: composers, singers, conductors, and operas and opera companies, among others. Many classical and concert musicians of the Harlem Renaissance appear. Among them are William Grant Still, Roland Hayes, Paul Robeson, and Marian Anderson. The book features a chronology of notable musical events, many of which occurred during the Harlem Renaissance. Looking at the chronology, one realizes that the Renaissance was a period of "firsts" for many opera and classical performers. Written for the general reader, this is a good source for students in grades 7 through 12.

Anderson, Marian. **My Lord, What a Morning**. Introduction by Nellie McKay. Madison, WI: The University of Wisconsin Press, 1992. Reprint. 348p. $37.50. ISBN 0-299-13390-7.

Anderson's autobiography was originally published in 1956. She writes of her childhood in Philadelphia, her studies, and her debut at Town Hall in New York during the Harlem Renaissance. Although the concert was a disaster, Anderson continued to work hard and finally achieved success. Anderson's book details many racial incidents throughout her life. One incident involved the denial of her entrance to a music school. Anderson merely recounts the incidents; her feelings are not revealed. Also, Anderson makes no mention of the political or social climate of the times in which she lived and worked. Despite the lack of such revelations, Anderson's book makes clear that she made many contributions to the concert world and undoubtedly paved the way for many other African Americans. McKay's introduction offers insights to what may seem like omissions on Anderson's part. McKay cites the qualities of dignity and humility that guided not only Anderson's writing, but her entire life. McKay also suggests that it is

Anderson's quality of dignity that made her victorious over those who sought to stop her. Recommended for adults and students in grades 7 through 12.

Arvey, Verna. **In One Lifetime: A Biography of William Grant Still**. Introduction by B. A. Nugent. Fayetteville, AR: University of Arkansas Press, 1984. 290p. $16.00. ISBN 0-938626-31-0.

William Grant Still's widow wrote this account of her husband's life. She provides insights into his growth as a composer, his writing, and his productions. She also writes of his childhood, his college years, and his life in New York. Still's life was not problem-free, and Arvey tells of his struggles with racism and professional jealousies and of his problems trying to get his work noticed. Arvey's work is obviously subjective, but it does offer an account of Still's life and of the struggles he faced. Written for adults, it can be read by students in grades 10 through 12 as well.

Duberman, Martin. **Paul Robeson: A Biography**. New York: Alfred A. Knopf, 1988. 816p. $17.95. ISBN 1-56584-288-X.

Duberman's biography is excellent for many reasons. Thoroughly researched, it provides an intimate portrait of Paul Robeson as a public figure and as a man. It includes details of Robeson's musical pursuits, along with more than 100 black-and-white photographs. This book also presents a social history of the times during which Robeson lived. The table of contents lists years covered after each chapter, enabling researchers to zero in on the time period of their choice. Written for adults, the author's highly readable narrative style makes this is an excellent source for students in grades 10 through 12 as well.

Ehrlich, Scott. **Paul Robeson**. Black Americans of Achievement Series. New York: Chelsea House, 1988. 111p. $19.95. ISBN 1-555-46-608-7.

Ehrlich's book, part of an excellent series of biographies of African Americans, presents Paul Robeson's career achievements and biographical facts. Included are details of Robeson's performances on stage and in film. Ehrlich provides much detail on Robeson's personal trials, which resulted from his efforts to overcome racial injustice. Several black-and-white photographs and a chronology of events in Robeson's life complete the book. Written for students in grades 7 through 10.

Floyd, Samuel. **Black Music in the Harlem Renaissance: A Collection of Essays**. No. 128 of Contributions in Afro-American Studies. Westport, CT: Greenwood, 1990. 228p. $45.00. ISBN 0-313-26546-1.

Beginning with Floyd's essay "Music in the Harlem Renaissance: An Overview," this volume offers various perspectives on the music of that time. Topics include essays on classical musicians, Black musical theatre, relationships between art and music and between writers and music, and vocal concert music. Floyd's essay touches on the conflict between the intellectuals, whom W. E. B. Du Bois called "The Talented Tenth," and popular music. Rawn Spearman's essay on vocal concert music traces the struggles performers had to face and, in particular, discusses Roland Hayes's career. Rae Linda Brown's essay on classical musicians provides details on the career and music of William Grant Still, as well as lesser-known composers Florence Price and William Dawson. Also included is a bibliography of concert music of Harlem Renaissance composers from 1919–35. This book is not intended for young adults, but the information here is not found in other sources. This book is recommended for students in grades 10 through 12.

Floyd, Samuel, Jr., and Marsha J. Reisser. **Black Music Biography: An Annotated Bibliography**. White Plains, NY: Kraus International, 1987. 302p. ISBN 0-527-30158-2.

The authors have compiled an annotated bibliography of biographies of several Harlem Renaissance-era musicians. Among them are Marian Anderson, R. Nathaniel Dett, and William Grant Still. Each work is annotated with reviews and a discography. This book is not available from the publisher at this time, and many sources listed in it may be out of print. The authors, however, suggest that their work could be used as a series of vignettes because annotations provide personal and professional highlights. They read like short narratives. The introduction lists performers in chronological order, making it easy to single out Harlem Renaissance artists. Recommended for students in grades 10 through 12 and adults.

Gray, James, comp. **Blacks in Classical Music: A Bibliographical Guide to Composers, Performers, and Ensembles**. No. 15 of Music Reference Collection Series. Westport, CT: Greenwood, 1988. 298p. $55.00. ISBN 0-313-26056-7.

Grey begins his work with a general section of bibliographies, then continues with specific categories such as "Composers," "Symphony Artists," and "Concert and Opera Singers." The volume covers everything written by or about the performers. Entries are numbered. Many of the Harlem Renaissance musicians are listed here, including William Grant Still, Roland Hayes, Paul Robeson, and Marian Anderson. Written for the researcher, this book is also an appropriate source for student researchers in grades 10 through 12.

Haskins, James. "Marian Anderson." In **One More River to Cross**. New York: Scholastic, 1992. 215p. $3.50. ISBN 0-590-42897-7.

Haskins devotes a section of this book, written about individuals who were victims of what Haskins calls "institutional racism," to Marian Anderson. Anderson struggled to study classical music and overcame many obstacles, including racism. Her inspiring story is told by Haskins in a clear and dramatic style. He successfully mixes biographical facts with his message. This book is written for students in grades 7 through 12.

———. "William Grant Still." In **Black Music in America: A History Through Its People**. New York: HarperCollins, 1987. 224p. $15.89. ISBN 0-690-04462-3.

Haskins traces Black music in America from slavery to the present. Chapter 5 begins with commentary on the Harlem Renaissance. Pages 96 through 102 consist of a profile of William Grant Still. The book is well written and provides details of Still's personal life and career. A black-and-white photograph is also included. Haskins's work is widely respected, and he is considered an authority in the field of Black studies. This work is written for students in grades 7 through 12.

Larsen, Rebecca. **Paul Robeson: Hero Before His Time**. New York: Franklin Watts, 1989. 158p. $15.33. ISBN 0-531-10779-5.

In this in-depth study of Paul Robeson's life, Larsen emphasizes equally his professional career and his political activities. Larsen, a reporter, includes excerpts from many documents, letters, and speeches. Her background in journalism is evident: Her writing is clear and straightforward, and the book is well researched. She examines in detail Robeson's struggles against racism and his stand against injustice. Written especially for students in grades 7 through 10.

Patterson, Charles. **Marian Anderson**. Impact Biography Series. New York: Franklin Watts, 1988. 160p. $15.47. ISBN 0-531-10568-7.

This is a well-written biography of Marion Anderson's life. In addition to describing her childhood, her training, and her career, the book details her efforts to overcome prejudice. Photographs are included, as well as a chronology of important events in her life. Patterson's writing is straightforward and engaging and will appeal to students in grades 7 through 10.

Robeson, Paul. **A Lonesome Road**. London: ASV Living Era, 1994. Audiocassette.

Robeson recorded the selections on this tape between 1925 and 1932 in England. The selections include spirituals and traditional music, as well as "Ol' Man River" from *Showboat*, a musical in which Robeson appeared. Also included is "Steal Away," one of the first songs Robeson recorded. Robeson's voice is powerful and soulful. Recommended for all ages.

Smith, Eric Ledell. **Blacks in Opera: An Encyclopedia of People and Companies, 1873–1993**. Cleveland, OH: New Day Press, 1993. 272p. $49.95. ISBN 0-913678-13-9.

Smith's work is actually a biographical dictionary. Personal entries include dates, debuts, roles, awards, and recordings, as well as other pertinent information. Entries for companies include dates, founder, location, and members. This book also features black-and-white photographs. It lists "firsts" for black opera singers and composers, many of which occurred during the Harlem Renaissance. Recommended for anyone interested in opera or Black studies.

Southern, Eileen. **The Music of Black Americans: A History**. New York: W. W. Norton, 1971. 552p. $21.95. ISBN 393-02156-4.

Part 4, "Lift Every Voice and Sing," is devoted to the music of the Harlem Renaissance. Southern profiles major musicians of the era, including Eva Jessye, concert singer. She also discusses lesser-known performers. Black-and-white photographs complement the text. Recommended for adults and students in grades 10 through 12.

Tedards, Ann. **Marian Anderson**. American Women of Achievement Series. New York: Chelsea House, 1988. 112p. $17.95. ISBN 1-55546-638-9.

Tedards, herself a professional singer, puts her musical background to good use in this well-researched and clearly written book. Chapters 1 and 2 are significant to those interested in the Harlem Renaissance. They trace Anderson's childhood in Philadelphia, the support she received from Roland Hayes, her success performing in Harlem, and her experiences with racism. The book features an excellent selection of black-and-white photographs, a chronology of significant events in Anderson's career, and a bibliography. Written for students in grades 7 through 10.

Turner, Patricia. **Dictionary of Afro-American Performers: 78 RPM and Other Cylindrical Recordings of Opera, Choral Music and Song, 1900–1949**. New York: Garland, 1990. 433p. ISBN 0-8240-8736-4.

Although out of print at this time, Turner's work is an important resource as it fills a gap left by other discographies; Turner's work is a compilation of African American performers. This book is an excellent source of information on classical musicians of the Harlem Renaissance. Individual entries consist of a short biography, a bibliography, and a discography.

Marion Anderson, Roland Hayes, Paul Robeson, and William Grant Still are all profiled here. This is a good source for locating recordings, many of which have been reissued. Written for the music scholar, but easily used by students in grades 10 through 12 as well.

Fig. 15.1.
"Peg Leg" Bates (Schomburg Center, NYPL).

Dance and Dancers

Dance is an essential element of African American culture. Some of the most talented dancers in history performed during the Harlem Renaissance. Most famous was Bill Robinson. He was so popular during the Renaissance that he was called the "Mayor of Harlem." Clayton "Peg Leg" Bates was another tap dance legend. Elida Webb was noted not only for dance, but for her choreography.

The Dance Craze

A variety of dances originated during the Harlem Renaissance, including the Charleston, the Black Bottom, the Shim Sham Shimmy, and the Lindy Hop. The Charleston became a dance craze, with Elida Webb, choreographer for the Broadway show *Runnin' Wild*, introducing it in the show. The dance steps involve gyrations with the legs and arms, and the dance has become classic.

The Black Bottom, another popular dance, originated in the Broadway show *Dinah*. It involved turning and moving back and forth and slapping the hand on the buttocks. It, too, became popular during the Harlem Renaissance.

These dances may have originated in shows, but dancing was a craze all over America during the Harlem Renaissance. Many Whites flocked uptown to Harlem dance halls to learn the latest steps and to watch Harlemites in action. The most notable dance hall was the Savoy Ballroom, known as "The Home of Happy Feet," and many dances originated there as well, including the Lindy Hop, an energetic jitterbug dance involving a series of steps with intermittent twirls, spins, and splits. The Shim Sham Shimmy, which had dancers freeze in place, was yet another Savoy creation.

Clayton "Peg Leg" Bates

Clayton Bates, born in the rural South, lost his leg at the age of 10 in a cotton gin accident. His uncle made a peg leg for him, and Bates started dancing by imitating his uncle. Bates soon discovered that he could do things with his peg that other dancers could not do, and his career began. He arrived in New York during the Harlem Renaissance and became a hit. After a long and successful career, he retired and became a successful entrepreneur.

Bill Robinson

Robinson was born in Richmond, Virginia, in the late 1870s. He demonstrated his talent for dancing when he was still a child. His career began in vaudeville. During the Harlem Renaissance, Robinson appeared on Broadway and became a hit. He was known for his staircase dance, which involved his dancing up and down a staircase. On each step, the tempo and dance steps were changed. Although Robinson projected a smiling face and happy demeanor, he had many troubles in his life. He made several Hollywood films later in his career.

Elida Webb

Elida Webb was both a dancer and choreographer. She made a name for herself as a dancer in *Shuffle Along*, the Broadway show that many believed was one of the catalysts of the Harlem Renaissance. She was then hired as choreographer for *Runnin' Wild*, the show that introduced the Charleston. For many years she worked at the Cotton Club as choreographer, the first African American to do so. Her later life is tinged with sadness, but she was an original and made many contributions to the field of dance.

Learn more about these and other dancers and dances of the Harlem Renaissance in the following sources.

Bibliography

Adamczyk, Alice J. **Black Dance: An Annotated Bibliography**. New York: Garland, 1989. 213p. ISBN 0-8240-8808-5.

All 1,400 entries in this volume are from various collections in the New York Public Library. Most of the book centers on African American dance in the United States over the past 50 years. However, there are photographs of and sources on performers popular during the Harlem Renaissance, including Bill Robinson and Peg Leg Bates. The book is intended for those researching African American dance. However, this reference is easy for students in grades 10 through 12 to use as well. This is an excellent starting point for research. The book is unavailable from the publisher, but because it is an important reference, it is worth seeking out.

Davidson, Dave, and Amber Edwards, prod. **The Dancing Man— Peg Leg Bates**. PBS Video, 1992. Videocassette, 60 min. $59.95. ISBN 0-7936-0742-6.

"Peg Leg" Bates led an extraordinary life. He overcame many obstacles, including the loss of a leg, to become one of the world's foremost tap dancers. At the time this film was made, Bates was 84 years old. He recounts career achievements from his time in vaudeville through his later years as an entrepreneur. Other personalities, including dancer Gregory Hines, add to this portrait of a Harlem Renaissance legend. Recommended for all ages and students of dance.

Emery, Lynne Fauley. **Black Dance from 1619 to Today**. 2d rev. ed. London: Dance Books, 1988. 397p. $19.95. ISBN 1-85273-005-6.
In this well-researched, well-written book, Emery traces the history of African American dance. Of particular interest to those researching dance during the Harlem Renaissance are chapter 7, "From Dance Hall to Theater," and chapter 8, "Concert Dance Pioneers: 1920–1950." In chapter 7, Emery defines dance halls and jook houses, and discusses Harlem nightclubs. She also discusses the shows *Shuffle Along* and *Runnin' Wild*. Emery profiles dancers of the era: Earl "Snakehips" Tucker, Florence Mills, Josephine Baker, and Bill Robinson. In chapter 8 she profiles Hemsley Winfield and Charlotte Kennedy, both concert dancers during the Harlem Renaissance. This information is not found in other sources. Included are black-and-white photographs and illustrations. Written for adults, but appropriate for students in grades 10 through 12 as well.

Haskins, James. **Black Dance in America: A History Through Its People**. New York: HarperCollins, 1990. 240p. $6.95. ISBN 0-06-446121-1.
Each chapter in this chronologically arranged book begins with an introduction that provides a historical perspective of the time period. The book offers information on significant dances, dancers, and organizations. Chapter 3 details dance during the Harlem Renaissance. It also includes background on the Charleston, a profile of Elida Webb, and profiles of Bill Robinson and Clarence "Buddy" Bradley. Chapter 4 focuses on the 1930s, although pages 87 through 90 offer a profile of Clayton "Peg Leg" Bates, a popular performer during the Harlem Renaissance. Haskins is an acclaimed writer of African American history and biography. Many of his books are written for students in grades 7 through 12, but they can be enjoyed by adults as well.

Haskins, James, and N. R. Mitgang. **Mr. Bojangles: The Biography of Bill Robinson**. New York: William Morrow, 1988. 336p. $17.95. ISBN 0-688-07203-8.
This book is the most thorough source on Bill Robinson found at this time. Although Robinson, nicknamed the "Mayor of Harlem," was highly visible during the Harlem Renaissance, his career spanned several decades. Robinson began dancing on the vaudeville circuit, moved on to Broadway, and finally starred in Hollywood films. Haskins and Mitgang thoroughly researched Robinson's professional career and personal life. They also interviewed several of his friends and contemporaries. The result is a detailed portrait of Robinson not found in other sources. The authors look past the smiling facade to reveal the serious side of their subject. Anecdotes provide added details and personal glimpses of Robinson's relationships. One interesting aspect of Robinson's life as a resident of Harlem is his relationship with the New York City Police Department. Several black-and-white photographs enhance the text. Chapters 4 through 8 cover specifically the time period of the Harlem Renaissance. Written for adults, this book is also appropriate for students in grades 7 through 12.

Long, Richard T. **The Black Tradition in American Dance**. New York: Smithmark, 1995. 192p. $19.98. ISBN 0-8317-0763-1.

Long begins his work with an overview of early African American musical theatre, African American dancers, and buck dancing. In chapter 2, he focuses on concert dance, theatre, and dance halls. This chapter will be of interest to those researching the Harlem Renaissance because Long's discussion is limited to the years 1920–36, roughly the period of the Harlem Renaissance. Long provides information on Florence Mills and Josephine Baker, dance halls, nightclubs, Broadway shows, and vaudeville, which was still popular during the Harlem Renaissance. Also included is a chronology, which begins in 1920. This is not as comprehensive a source as some others, but the color photographs and reproductions make it nonetheless worthwhile. Recommended for adults and students in grades 7 through 12.

Thorpe, Edward. **Black Dance**. New York: Overlook Press, 1994. 192p. $19.95. ISBN 0-87951-563-5.

As with other sources, this book traces the history of dance and profiles many dancers. Chapters 12 through 18 relate to the period of the Harlem Renaissance. In addition to discussing jazz, dance halls, and Broadway shows, Thorpe traces the origins of dances popular in the 1920s: the Black Bottom and the Charleston. Thorpe also presents a discussion of tap dancing, which is not found in other sources. Several black and white photographs are included, some of which depict dancers at the Savoy Ballroom. This is not a comprehensive resource, but Thorpe covers various elements of dance. Recommended for adults and students in grades 7 through 12.

Zuber, Shari Lyn. "Charleston!" **Cobblestone** 12, no. 2 (February 1991): 31–33.

Zuber's article gives a brief background of the Charleston. She also mentions other dances popular during the Harlem Renaissance that originated at the Savoy Ballroom. She provides explicit, step-by-step instructions and illustrations on how to do the Charleston, although she does not list sources of music to dance to. This is a worthwhile article for those interested in learning the dance that was part of the dance craze during the Roaring Twenties. Written for readers in grades 4 through 9, the article is informative and can be enjoyed by all ages.

Theatre

Theatre flourished during the Harlem Renaissance. Notable performers included Charles Gilpin, who made history in the title role of Eugene O'Neill's *The Emperor Jones*. Another O'Neill play, *All God's Chillun Got Wings*, starred Paul Robeson, who became world renowned not only for his acting and singing talent, but also for his political beliefs. The most notable theatre experience of the Harlem Renaissance was the opening of *Shuffle Along*. It has been credited as having marked the beginning of the Harlem Renaissance. Many theatre groups flourished as well. Among the most famous were The Lafayette Players Stock company.

Find out more about theatre and those who performed during the Harlem Renaissance in these references.

Bibliography

Duberman, Martin. **Paul Robeson: A Biography**. New York: Alfred A. Knopf, 1996. 816p. $17.95. ISBN 1-56584-288-X.

Duberman's biography is excellent for many reasons. It is thoroughly researched, providing an intimate portrait of Robeson as public figure and as a man. Duberman's writing is clear and engaging. The book also presents a social history of the times during which Robeson lived, including the Harlem Renaissance. Robeson appeared in several theatre productions during the Harlem Renaissance. More than 100 black-and-white photographs have been included. The table of contents lists years covered in each chapter, enabling those interested in the period of the Harlem Renaissance to locate them easily. Written for adults, this is an excellent source for students in grades 10 through 12 as well.

Ehrlich, Scott. **Paul Robeson**. Black Americans of Achievement Series. New York: Chelsea House, 1988. 111p. $19.95. ISBN 1-55546-608-7.

Part of an excellent series of biographies of African Americans, Ehrlich's book mixes biographical facts with career achievements. He provides much detail on Robeson's personal trials, which resulted from his courageous efforts to achieve racial equality, but he traces his theatrical pursuits as well. The book includes a chronology and bibliography, along with several black-and-white photographs. This is a biography specifically written for students in grades 7 through 10.

Flowers, H. D., II. **Blacks in American Theatre History: Images, Realities, Potential**. 2d ed. Edina, MN: Burgess International Group, 1993. 208p. $21.95. ISBN 0-8087-3062-2.

Arranged chronologically, Flowers's work traces the history of African American theatre. Chapter 2, "White Playwrights and Negro Characters," presents summaries and analyses of plays, such as *The Emperor Jones*, *Porgy*, and *In Abraham's Bosom*. Flowers also defines stereotypes of African Americans in these dramas. In chapter 5, "The Black Actor," the author briefly profiles Charles Gilpin, Rose McClendon, and Paul Robeson. Other chapters provide information on the Lafayette Theatre and the Negro Little Theatre Movement, both active during the Harlem Renaissance. Included are several black-and-white photographs and a chronology. Appropriate for students in grades 10 through 12 and adults.

Johnson, Helen Armstead. "Shuffle Along: Keynote of the Harlem Renaissance." In **The Theatre of Black Americans: A Collection of Critical Essays**. Edited by Errol Hill. New York: Applause Theatre Book Publishers, 1990. 374p. $14.95. ISBN 0-936839-27-9.

Johnson, founder and director of the Armstead Johnson Foundation for Theatre Research, an organization devoted to collecting and preserving materials related to African American contributions to theatre, has written a comprehensive essay about *Shuffle Along*. She includes reviews of the show; a brief overview of African American theatre before and during the Harlem Renaissance; profiles of performers, writers, and producers of the show; and a plot summary. The essay is informative and clearly written. Intended for adults, but students in grades 10 through 12 will benefit from it as well.

Larsen, Rebecca. **Paul Robeson: Hero Before His Time**. New York: Franklin Watts, 1989. 158p. $15.33. ISBN 0-531-10779-5.

In this in-depth study of Paul Robeson's life, Larsen emphasizes equally his career and his political activities. Larsen, a reporter, includes excerpts from many documents, letters, and speeches. Her background in journalism is evident: Her writing is straightforward, and the book is well researched. She examines in detail Robeson's struggles against racism and his stand against injustice. Written especially for students in grades 7 through 10.

Shaw, Arnold. "Shuffle Along." In **Black Popular Music in America: From the Spirituals, Minstrels, and Ragtime to Soul, Disco, and Hip Hop**. New York: Schirmer Books, 1986, 386p. $21.95. ISBN 0-02872310-4.

Shaw includes a section on Black Stock Companies in this chapter. It provides a great deal of information on *Shuffle Along*. This is a good source for historical information on the show and some popular performers of the Harlem Renaissance. It also presents a social history of the period. Written in an engaging style, the book includes biographical information, as well as bibliographies and discographies for each chapter. This book is written for adults, but it is also suitable for students in grades 7 through 12.

Thompson, Sister Francesca, O.S.F. "The Lafayette Players, 1915–1932." In **The Theatre of Black Americans: A Collection of Critical Essays**. Edited by Errol Hill. New York: Applause Theatre Book Company, 1990. 374p. $14.95. ISBN 0-936839-27-9.

Thompson's essay, on pages 211 through 230, traces the origins of the Lafayette Players theatre company. It provides specific details on its founder, Anita Bush, who struggled to make a name for the group. It further discusses how the Lafayette Players developed into a first-rate theatre company and the company's closing, which was brought about by the Great Depression. Sr. Thompson discusses the significance of the Players in the history of theatre of African Americans and cites productions put on by the company. This essay provides an inside look at one of the best and most widely known theatre groups of the Harlem Renaissance. Written for adults, this book is also suitable for students in grades 10 through 12.

Woll, Allen. **Dictionary of the Black Theater: Broadway, Off-Broadway, and Selected Harlem Theater**. Westport, CT: Greenwood, 1983. 360p. $49.95. ISBN 0-313-22561-3.

Woll begins his introduction with a history of Black theatre. He makes mention of many Harlem Renaissance-era productions. In part 1, Woll provides an alphabetical list of shows with all pertinent information: opening date, theatre, number of performances, creative personnel, cast credits, songs, plot summary, and critical review. Part 2 consists of a dictionary of personalities and organizations. Also included is a chronology of African American theatre. The Harlem Renaissance is well represented. Appendixes include a discography and a bibliography. Indexes are by name, play and film, and song. This book is written for adults, but is appropriate for students in grades 10 through 12 as well.

Part VI
Sports and Entertainment

Sports

Although artistic expression was the hallmark of the Harlem Renaissance, athletic accomplishments were also a part of this era. As the Harlem Renaissance was a cultural movement that focused on the achievements of all African Americans, it seems appropriate to examine those achievements from the arena of athletics as well. Among notable athletes were Olympians Ralph Metcalfe, Eddie Tolan, and Dehart Hubbard. Two basketball teams popular at the time were the Harlem Globetrotters and the Renaissance Big Five, also known as the Rens. Black baseball leagues were also very active. Although many of the baseball achievements of this time did not take place in New York, much less in Harlem, several teams did represent New York during the 1920s. By 1926, Negro Leagues had been organized, and a Negro World Series was played in Kansas City, Missouri. Also worth examining are the life and career of Jack Johnson. Johnson's boxing career reached its peak prior to the Renaissance, but he still managed to make headlines until his death in 1946.

Use the following sources to discover more about these famous athletes.

Bibliography

Ashe, Arthur. **A Hard Road to Glory: A History of the African American Athlete 1919–1945**. Vol. 2 of Hard Road to Glory Series. New York: Warner Books, 1988. 497p. $89.95. ISBN 0-446-71007-5.

Ashe's work traces the history of eight different sports. The introduction discusses events significant in the history of African American athletics: the Great Migration, formation of the Negro National Leagues, and formation of the Rens and Globetrotters. Ashe's work—three volumes in all—has been thoroughly researched. Ashe interviewed several athletes and their contemporaries; they provided several anecdotes that make this an appealing source. In addition to professional and career highlights, Ashe supplies personal information on each athlete. Because Ashe presents a historical perspective throughout, his work reads like a social history of sports. The book is excellently detailed and clearly written, with information that is not found elsewhere. The Harlem Globetrotters, Rens, and Olympians Dehart Hubbard, Eddie Tolan, and Ralph Metcalfe are all covered. Several black-and-white photographs enhance the text. An extensive reference section and a bibliography, as well as collegiate and regional sports information, round out the book. Recommended for adults and students in grades 7 through 12.

Chalk. Ocania. **Pioneers of Black Sport**. New York: Dodd, Mead, 1975. 305p. ISBN 0-396-06868-5.

Chalk's work is arranged by sport: baseball, basketball, boxing, and football. Chalk provides a good deal of information on these sports. Of particular interest is the section on basketball. The author includes much information on the Renaissance Big Five, also known as the Rens, a popular basketball team in Harlem and one of the best ever. Chalk also includes several black-and-white photographs amd team profiles. There is a small amount of information on the Harlem Globetrotters. Recommended for adults and students in grades 7 through 12.

Davis, Lenwood G., and Belinda Daniels, comp. **Black Athletes in the United States: A Bibliography of Books, Articles, Autobiographies, and Biographies of Black Professional Athletes in the United States, 1800–1981**. Westport, CT: Greenwood, 1981. 228p. $65.00. ISBN 0-313-22976-7.

Davis and Daniels arranged this bibliography by type of book or article. It includes books by and about professional athletes. Appendixes list those in the Hall of Fame of a particular sport, Most Valuable Players, records, and films about Black athletes or in which they appeared. The book lists three films in which Jack Johnson appeared during the Harlem Renaissance. Of particular interest are the headlines of newspaper articles covering Johnson's career and private life; they reflect the White attitude toward Blacks at the time. Designed for researchers, this book is fairly easy to access. Therefore, it is suitable for students in grades 10 through 12.

Heath, George D. "The Rens." **Cobblestone** 12, no. 2 (February 1991): 40–41.

Heath's article traces the history of the New York Renaissance, also known as the Rens or the Renaissance Big Five. Although the article is brief, Heath provides details of games, wins and losses, and a picture of the team. The Rens were one of the best teams ever; at one point they had an 88-game winning streak. This is one of the few sources of information and photographs of the Rens. Published for grades 4 through 9, the article is appropriate for readers in grades 10 through 12 as well.

McKissack, Patricia C., and Fredrick McKissack Jr. **Black Diamond: The Story of the Negro Baseball Leagues**. New York: Scholastic, 1994. 192p. $13.95. ISBN 0-590-45809-4.

The McKissacks are widely respected, award-winning young adult authors. They trace the history of African Americans in baseball as early as 1867 to the present day. Well documented and well written, the book is full of fascinating details. It includes several black-and-white photographs, a "Profiles" section, and a "Time Line," which not only lists important events in baseball but also provides information on national events. Using the index enables readers to zero in on baseball in New York during the Harlem Renaissance. Excellent reading for all ages.

Page, James. **Black Olympian Medalists**. Englewood, CO: Libraries Unlimited, 1991. 190p. $27.50. ISBN 0-87287-618-7.

Alphabetically arranged entries for each subject include birth and death dates, event and medals won, and personal and career data. Further sources of information appear after each entry. Dehart Hubbard, Eddie Tolan, and Ralph Metcalfe are all discussed in this book. Year-by-year winners of events and medals won are listed in a chart in an appendix. This book should be especially appealing to readers in grades 7 through 12.

Porter, David L., ed. **African American Sports Greats: A Biographical Dictionary**. Westport, CT: Greenwood, 1995. 429p. $59.95. ISBN 0-313-28987-5.

Biographical profiles of more than 150 African American athletes include personal information and professional accomplishments. In addition, the preface contains a "History of African Americans in Professional and Olympic Sports." Appendixes list entries by name and by sport. Several black-and-white photographs are included. This is a good source for locating information on legendary athletes of the Harlem Renaissance. Written for students in grades 7 through 12.

Ritt, Martin, dir. **The Great White Hope**. Fox, 1970. Videocassette.

This excellent film traces the professional and personal life of boxer Jack Johnson. It depicts the treatment of Blacks by Whites in the years just prior to the Harlem Renaissance, thus providing insight into the injustice suffered by African Americans. It provides excellent background in social history and depicts the need for the movement toward racial equality, which was at the heart of the Harlem Renaissance. The film is true to the period, and the starring actors are excellent; both were nominated for Academy Awards. The film received an "R" rating, making it suitable for viewers ages 17 and older.

Rust, Edna, and Art Rust Jr. **Art Rust's Illustrated History of the Black Athlete**. Garden City, NY: Doubleday, 1985. 435p. $10.95. ISBN 0-385-15140-3.

Arrangement of this book is by sport. The authors' introduction not only traces the history of each sport but also examines the history of Black athletes involved in the sport. Sections include discussions of the Rens, the Globetrotters, and the Negro Leagues. Profiles of individual players on these teams and of Dehart Hubbard, Eddie Tolan, and Ralph Metcalfe are also included. The index provides easy access to the information. Photographs appear for each entrant as well as several for the team. This is an excellent sports reference book for readers of all ages.

Fig. 18.1.
The Apollo Theatre, 1930s (Schomburg Center, NYPL).

Apollo Theatre

The Apollo Theatre is a Harlem landmark. The theatre opened in the late 1920s during the decline of the Harlem Renaissance. It is famous for its shows, often featuring several headliners at one time. Winners were and still are judged by the audience, referred to by many as the toughest audience in the world. Amateur Night at the Apollo is still a popular feature; it has been broadcast on television for many years. Several legendary performers appeared at these talent contests early in their careers.

The Apollo was a special place during the last years of the Harlem Renaissance, just as it is today. Wallace Thurman's play *Harlem* premiered at the Apollo on February 20, 1929, before going on to Broadway. The Tree of Hope, a famous Harlem landmark during the 1920s and 1930s, was eventually chopped down, but its stump lives on at the Apollo.

Read about the Apollo in the following sources. (See also chapter 12, "Blues," chapter 13, "Jazz," and chapter 20, "Entertainers.")

Bibliography

Dempsey, Anne. "The Tree of Hope." **Cobblestone** 12, no. 2 (February 1991): 27.

Although this article is extremely brief, it does provide information on the Tree of Hope, an elm tree once located on Seventh Avenue. The entire issue of this magazine is dedicated to the Harlem Renaissance. It is written especially for students in grades 4 through 9 and is available from the publisher for $4.50.

Fox, Ted. "Harlem's Early Years—The Apollo Heritage." In **Showtime at the Apollo**. New York: Da Capo, 1993. 336p. $13.95. ISBN 0-306-80503-0.

Fox presents the story of the Apollo Theatre as told by those who performed there. Included are more than 150 black-and-white photographs. Chapter 1 is especially pertinent because, as the title suggests, it also provides a history of Harlem. Although the theatre opened just as the

Renaissance was coming to an end, this book is excellent for its social history of Harlem and the anecdotes about the performers. The story about Bessie Smith is especially amusing. Many musicians and entertainers of the Renaissance played at the Apollo, and their stories are truly an oral history of this great landmark. This book is written for adults, but is recommended for students in grades 7 through 12 as well.

Schiffman, Jack. "Harlem Comes of Age." In **Uptown: The Story of Harlem's Apollo Theatre**. New York: Cowles, 1971. 210p. ISBN 0-402-12062-0.

Although this book is more than 25 years old and out of print, it is included here because its author, Jack Schiffman, is the son of the man who created the Apollo. "Harlem Comes of Age" (pages 45–69) is devoted to performers who appeared at the Apollo during the 1930s and 1940s. Those who performed in the early 1930s should be of interest to anyone researching the Harlem Renaissance. As someone who literally grew up at the Apollo, Schiffman's personal reminiscences make this a lively and entertaining source. Schiffman's anecdotes add a personal perspective to the profiles of those who performed there. Recommended for adults and students in grades 7 through 12.

Fig. 19.1.
Cotton Club Interior (Schomburg Center, NYPL).

Cotton Club

Nightclubs were an important facet of life in Harlem during the Harlem Renaissance. Jazz was the latest craze in music, and Whites were flocking uptown to listen. Connie's Inn, Small's Paradise, Pod's and Jerry's, and Tillie's Chicken Shack were among the many popular clubs that flourished during the Harlem Renaissance.

The Cotton Club, however, was the most legendary of all night spots. Nationwide radio broadcasts made the club famous all over the United States. Many great performers achieved national recognition as a result of working at the Cotton Club, which was owned by White gangster Owney Madden. The club was restricted to White customers, but all performers were Black.

Learn why the Cotton Club and its performers became legendary. See also chapter 13, "Jazz," to find out about legendary bandleaders Duke Ellington and Fletcher Henderson, whose orchestras were both house bands at the Cotton Club.

Bibliography

Calloway, Cab, and Bryant Rollins. **Of Minnie the Moocher and Me**. New York: Thomas Y. Crowell, 1976. 282p. ISBN 0-690-01032-X.
Calloway's book is out of print, but it is an important source for its content about the Cotton Club during the Harlem Renaissance. Calloway and his orchestra became the house band at the Cotton Club after Duke Ellington's and Fletcher Henderson's runs there. His autobiography tells of his troubled early life and his introduction to music. Calloway also provides several career highlights. Among the most interesting are his memories of working at the Cotton Club during the Harlem Renaissance. Written in a conversational style, the book has many humorous anecdotes. Calloway was flamboyant, and this is evident not only in the black-and-white photographs but in his writing. Written for adults, this book should also appeal to students in grades 7 through 12. Excerpts from the book can be found in *Reading Jazz*, edited by Robert Gottlieb (listed below).

Gottlieb, Robert, ed. **Reading Jazz: A Gathering of Autobiography, Reportage, and Criticism from 1919 to Now**. New York: Pantheon, 1996. 1,088p. $40.00. ISBN 0-679-4425-1-0.

Gottlieb's work is organized in three sections: autobiography, reportage, and criticism. It contains a wealth of information on jazz, with a number of selections from the era of the Harlem Renaissance. Included in the autobiography section are excerpts from Cab Calloway's autobiography. Also included is an excerpt of Sidney Bechet's autobiography, another musician active during the Harlem Renaissance. Gottlieb's work is worth examining for these sections, alone. Recommended for adults and students in grades 10 through 12.

Haskins, James. **The Cotton Club**. rev. ed. New York: Hippocrene Books, 1994. 213p. $14.95. ISBN 0-7818-0248-2.

Haskins opens with a brief history of Harlem. Details include the Great Migration, the evolution of business and nightlife in Harlem, and the creativity that permeated Harlem. This creativity is what set the stage for White interest in the "New Negro." Several black-and-white photographs and illustrations are included, as well as a bibliography and reminiscences of performers, reporters, and customers. Also included are various quotations from Langston Hughes. Haskins provides details not only of legendary musicians but also of shows, revues, and lesser-known acts. Haskins, a prolific author, has produced a highly readable, thoroughly researched book for adults and students in grades 7 through 12.

Stone, Andrew, dir. **Stormy Weather**. Fox, 1943. Videocassette.

Although this film was made long after the decline of the Harlem Renaissance, it is worth seeing because all of its major stars performed at the Cotton Club during that time. This all-Black musical features Cab Calloway and his orchestra, Lena Horne, Fats Waller, Bill Robinson, and the Nicholas Brothers, all of whom perform numbers made famous during the Harlem Renaissance. There is a story line to the film, but the performances are what makes the film memorable. Selections include "Ain't Misbehavin'," "Digga Digga Do," and "Basin Street Blues." This movie was made before the rating system, but this film is pure entertainment, making it appropriate for students in grades 7 through 12.

Fig. 20.1.
Josephine Baker (Schomburg Center, NYPL).

Entertainers

Many entertainers popular during the Harlem Renaissance cannot be categorized. Not all performed at the Cotton Club, nor was their work classified as jazz or classical music or theatre. (See also chapter 13, "Cotton Club.") Although many entertainers did perform at the Cotton Club, they also appeared at other clubs, in revues and shows. Many were hits on Broadway. One such performer was Josephine Baker, who spent most of her life in Paris. Florence Mills and Ethel Waters were two other multitalented entertainers during the Harlem Renaissance.

Josephine Baker

Josephine Baker was born in St. Louis, Missouri, and danced in vaudeville as a child. At the age of 15, she was in the chorus of *Shuffle Along*. She soon became a sensation on Broadway, but an offer to star in a revue in Paris changed the course of her life. Baker stayed in Paris and became a star of the Folies Bergère. She was known for her dancing, especially her energetic performance of the Charleston and the Black Bottom. In time she added singing to her act. Baker was truly charismatic. Her personal life is fascinating as well: During World War II, she was a spy for the French government, for which she was awarded the French Legion of Honor, the country's highest honor.

Florence Mills

Florence Mills made her stage debut at the age of four and worked in show business her entire life. She was a star in *Shuffle Along*, causing a sensation every night when she sang. She appeared in many revues and shows and also toured Europe. She was truly an international star. Mills was multitalented and loved by her many fans. Unfortunately, she died tragically at the height of her career when she was only 26 years old.

Ethel Waters

Ethel Waters was born in Chester, Pennsylvania. Life was hard for a child living in the red-light district. She left home as soon as she could and began singing in Baltimore; however, she quickly moved to New York. She was known as "Sweet Mama Stringbean" and sang seductive songs when she appeared at the Cotton Club, on Broadway, and at several other Harlem nightclubs. Later in her career, she worked as an actress in movies and television. Waters was nominated for an Academy Award in 1950.

Use the following sources to find out more about entertainers of the Harlem Renaissance.

Bibliography

Carter, Lawrence T. **Eubie Blake: Keys of Memory**. Detroit, MI: Balamp Press, 1979. 116p. ISBN 0-913642-10-X.

Carter begins his book by describing his impressions of Eubie Blake and his home; Blake was living in Brooklyn at the time. The remainder of the book consists of Blake's reminiscences about his life. Several anecdotes told by Blake occurred in New York at the time of the Harlem Renaissance. Blake counts among his friends stride piano players Willie "the Lion" Smith and James P. Johnson, as well as Caspar Holstein, another familiar figure in Harlem during the 1920s. Blake provides intimate details of how he and Noble Sissle put *Shuffle Along* on Broadway. His personality shines through in this delightful narrative. A thoroughly enjoyable book, it is recommended for adults and students in grades 7 through 12.

Estell, Kenneth, ed. "Performing Arts." In Vol. 4 of **Reference Library of Black America**. Detroit, MI: Gale Research, 1993. 1,600p. $179.90. ISBN 0-685-49222-2.

As with other volumes in the set, volume 4 opens with an essay that focuses on historical perspectives and ends with an extensive bibliography and an index. One section highlights African American performance artists from 1920 to 1960. Much of this section provides information about artists popular during the Harlem Renaissance, such as Josephine Baker, Florence Mills, Fats Waller, and Ethel Waters. Black-and-white photographs are included. This almanac is written especially for students in grades 7 through 12.

Hill, Anthony D. **Pages from the Harlem Renaissance: A Chronicle of Performance**. Vol. 6 of Studies in African and African American Culture Series. New York: Peter Lang, 1996. 186p. $29.95. ISBN 0-8204-2864-7.

Hill begins his work with a profile of J. A. Jackson, whose column appeared in *Billboard*, the national show business tabloid, during the 1920s. Illustrations include reproductions of "The Page," as Jackson's column was called; an entire chapter consists of reproductions and illustrations of the column. Additional topics include a chapter on the Black vaudeville circuit. Hill discusses the establishment of the Theatre Owners and Booking Association, provides maps of the circuit, and examines the issues that developed as a result. The Colored Actors Union is discussed as well. Appendixes include lists of performers, film companies, vaudeville acts, and theatres. A bibliography of books and dissertations rounds out the volume. Hill's subject matter is unique and he brings to light little-known details of African American performance history. Recommended for adults, but students in grades 10 through 12 can also use this reference.

Hughes, Langston, and Milton Meltzer. **Black Magic: A Pictorial History of African Americans in Performing Arts**. New York: Da Capo, 1990. Reprint. 384p. $19.95. ISBN 0-306-80406-9.

This work was originally published in 1967, shortly after Hughes's death. Arranged chronologically by topic, this single volume spans 300 years of the history of African American entertainers. Illustrations accompany the text. Written in narrative form, the book presents sketches of individuals as they relate to the topic or era. It is literally a photographic history. The table of contents includes chapters on dancers, Broadway, the Apollo Theatre, and composers. A subject index concludes the book. Both authors are highly respected. Hughes was a major force in the Harlem Renaissance, and Meltzer is an acclaimed biographer. Both have also written for young people. This volume should be especially appealing to students in grades 7 through 12.

Mapp, Edward. **Directory of Blacks in the Performing Arts**. 2d. ed. Metuchen, NJ: Scarecrow Press, 1990. 612p. $57.50. ISBN 0-8108-2222-9.

Mapp has produced a number of other African American references. In this one, entries are listed in alphabetical order and include name, brief relevant personal information, career data, and awards. The book also contains a bibliography and a list of organizations related to the entertainment industry and African American involvement in it. A classified index lists subjects according to field of endeavor. Performers described in this book who were active during the Harlem Renaissance include Bill Robinson, Ethel Waters, Josephine Baker, and Fats Waller. There are no illustrations, but the directory is both easy to read and highly interesting. Written for adults, it is also a good source for students in grades 10 through 12.

Schroeder, Alan. **Josephine Baker**. Black Americans of Achievement Series. New York: Chelsea House, 1991. 128p. $17.95. ISBN 0-7910-1116-X.

Written in clear, straightforward language, this biography traces Josephine Baker's life and career. From approximately 1922 through 1925, Baker appeared in many shows in New York, including *Shuffle Along*. She was an immediate hit before going to Paris in 1925. This book provides many details and photographs of the pre-Paris period of her career. The many black-and-white photographs enhance this description of Baker's fascinating life. They show, in particular, the many facets of Baker's talent. This book is part of an excellent series written for students in grades 7 through 10.

Waller, Maurice, and Anthony Calabrese. **Fats Waller**. Foreword by Michael Lipskin. New York: Macmillan General Reference, 1997. 231p. $15.00. ISBN 0028648854.

Fats Waller was a popular entertainer who performed at various clubs and cabarets during the Harlem Renaissance. He was known for his humor and his talent as a stride piano player. Although this book is out of print, it is worth looking for. Written by Waller's son, it is a well-documented account of Waller's private and public life. Waller recalls incidents in his family life, his father's encounters with racism, and relationships with other entertainers. The book also discusses Waller's music at length. Written for adults, but also appropriate for students in grades 10 through 12.

Waters, Ethel. With Charles Samuels. **His Eye Is on the Sparrow**.
Westport, CT: Greenwood, 1978. Reprint. 304p. $13.95. ISBN
0-306-80477-8.

Ethel Waters was a popular performer on Broadway, at the Cotton
Club, and later in films and on television. The song "Stormy Weather" was
written for her by George Gershwin. She writes in detail about these events
in her life. She also traces her childhood of poverty and violence, and tells
how she saw her way out of it by winning singing contests, working in
vaudeville, and finally achieving success in New York during the Harlem
Renaissance. Included as well are remembrances of her colleagues. Several
black-and-white photographs complement the text. Written for adults, this
book is also appropriate for students in grades 10 through 12.

Wright, Laurie. **"Fats" in Fact**. Essex, England: Storyville, 1992.
552p. ISBN 0-902391-14-3.

Wright has compiled a comprehensive work on Fats Waller. As the title
suggests, Wright set out to separate fact from fiction surrounding Waller's
life. The book opens with an excerpt in Waller's own words. Wright then
presents a biography and discography. Notes, information, and reminiscences are interspersed with the discography, making it uniquely more
interesting than most. Wright has included a section of piano rolls made by
Waller and a section called "The Miscellaneous Fats Waller." This is also full
of bits of information about Fats. Ernie Anderson, who promoted Fats
Waller's Carnegie Hall concert, and Courtney Williams, a former band
member, each wrote memoirs of their experiences with Waller. Several
black-and-white photographs are included, as well as a "Scrapbook" of many
more photos. There are indexes of people and places, tune titles, record
catalogs, and even a section of copyrights. This well-researched book is an
excellent source on Fats Waller. Appropriate for adults and students in
grades 10 through 12.

Zuber, Shari Lyn. "Entertainers of the Renaissance." **Cobblestone**
12, no. 2 (February 1991): 34–39.

Zuber's article provides a brief account of the period in the course of
describing Harlem nightlife. The article, though brief, features several
illustrations of entertainers, such as Florence Mills, Noble Sissle, Eubie
Blake, and the Nicholas Brothers. The text provides background on each
entertainer pictured. This article serves as a good introduction to the period.
Written in a publication produced for students in grades 4 through 7, this
article is appropriate for students in grades 10 through 12 as well.

Index

129